The Teenage Edge

Guiding Teens

to their Unique Strengths

by

Ted Warren

AWSNA

Printed with support from the Norton Foundation

Published by:
**The Association of Waldorf Schools
of North America
3911 Bannister Road
Fair Oaks, CA 95628**

Title: *The Teenage Edge*
    Guiding Teens to Their Unique Strengths
Author: Ted Warren
Editor: David Mitchell
Proofreaders, copyeditors: Nancy Jane and Donald Samson
Cover: Hallie Wootan
Cover Drawing: Heidi Skjerven
Illustrations: Ted Warren, Heidi Skjerven, and David Mitchell
© 2005 by AWSNA
ISBN # 1-888365-51-X

Contents

PART III
The Teenage Self

Foreword

The teenage years are a tremendous challenge for all of us. Teens push their edges in sports, in their relationships, and at school. They break rules and agreements! They are everything from rebellious to nasty to loving! Teens openly project their feelings onto the environment. They explode emotionally!

Underneath the explosiveness, teens are trying to discover the innovative aspects of their personality. They want to discover their Self, the core of their personality, their human being. The Self contains their temperament, their capacities and dispositions. Some call it the "authentic" Self. The Self uses the brain to think. Among many other activities it remembers, loves, suffers, experiences the world in pictures and it synthesizes sensory input. The Self also accesses the *Sense of Self* in order to reflect over its actions and to experience the Self of other people.

The emergence of the Self in the heart makes a teen unique. In their hearts they find their ideals, their goals and their insights. How to focus on the Self and support your teen along the way is the theme of this book.

What happens when this process is not nurtured by supportive adults who have a strong *Sense of Self*? What happens when it does? We will look at two different teenagers in depth and dozens more I have worked with over the years and note the difference in their development and what we, the caring adults in their lives, can do to enhance this important process.

My teenage years in Lackawanna County, Pennsylvania, on

the North Channel in Ontario, Canada, in Newport and Boston, led to an interest in education. I began my formal training in education at the Goetheanum outside of Basel, Switzerland in 1977 where I studied Waldorf Education and Anthroposophy, created by the Austrian scientist, Dr. Rudolf Steiner. My teacher and friend, Jørgen Smit, taught me the importance of the emerging Self and how to work with it in education. Between 1979 and 1997, I taught English and history to teens at the Waldorf School in Oslo, Norway.

The insights I offer in this book come from 25 years of research that I carried out while teaching full-time. I compared my experiences and theories with Freud, Jung, and Steiner, as well as many of their prominent followers today. Most importantly, my own three children, when teenagers themselves, continuously inspired and challenged me.

My work differs from most experts in that I consistently challenge teens to take themselves seriously by working actively with the key factors of their personality development. I always challenge teens to get to know their Self. I do this by teaching them what it is and how to recognize its existence within themselves. I then encourage them to take the Self seriously and to start integrating its unique qualities into their personality.

As a society obsessed with the cult of the personality, we often ignore the more subtle yet powerful potential of the Self. To a large extent we deny it completely! I am convinced that adults, schools, and other institutions that do not attempt to help teens search for the power of the Self are not helping young people bring forth their most valuable resource. During the years between thirteen and twenty, critical abilities are developed that will carry the teenager through an entire life. In the same way that supportive attitudes, independent thinking, and social initiatives create the teen's future, so do the unresolved personal issues continue to shape the quality of their lives. A young adult's healthy relationship to the Self can set some of the most disturbing influences from childhood and youth in their proper places.

In America there are roughly thirty-one million children between the ages of twelve and nineteen who daily explore new sides of their personalities. In the daily chaos they experience "the teenage edge," a natural but at times scary place in the personality of teens that helps define who they are. This edge contains both their unique strengths and their burning desire for experience. The "edge-experience" appears each time a teen engages the power of his or her emerging Self in actions. At such moments teens use their thinking, feeling or willing to create their own individual and unique futures.

On the edge they walk a fine line, because in one moment they are using the "edge experiences" in a constructive way, while in the next they can literally go over the edge and destroy parts of their lives. Both sides of the edge challenge teens tremendously. When they learn from their experiences, they put themselves back on track. If they block out experiences, they are at risk. It is in recognizing, and then dealing with, these "edge experiences" that adults can use the power of their own mature Self to give guidance and issue healthy challenges to their teens.

Being our greatest teachers, many teenagers speak for themselves in the following pages. The diary narrations by Carolin and Jason are fictionalized composites that represent very different aspects of how the Self emerges, but they are based on my parental and educational experiences. All other teens you will read about are individuals I have worked with in America and Norway, with some identifying details changed to protect their privacy.

This book is a work in progress. To share experiences and gain more knowledge, visit my website at:

http://www.teenage-edge.org

This book is a lifetime task and I have been blessed to receive the support and insight from many people. My deepest thanks go to David Mitchell and AWSNA Publications, and my literary agent Jake Elwell who for many years shared his knowledge and supported the project.

My editors Susan Schwarz and David Mitchell provided keen interest and sharp comments. My designer, Heidi Skjerven vitally portrayed the teenage edge.

A special thanks for their inspiration and support to Harold Cooper, Bo Ericsson, Lars Esholt, Dr. Jo Ellen Fischerkeller, Bent Flyen, Markus Jermann, Virginia Jordan, Jon McAlice, Eric McFadden, Nothart Rolfs, Robert Thomas, Marit Vaagen, Jon von Tetzchner, Valentin Wember, and Dr. Heinz Zimmermann.

I dedicate this book to my family Ragnhild, Erik, Siri and Christopher who gave me unconditional support and taught me how to guide teens.

PART I

The Teenage Years

Introduction

The teenage years are filled with contradictions, experimentation, passion, and rebellion. So much of what lies ahead is unknown. No doubt, the teenagers you are living and working with are going through dramatic and powerful changes. Much of their lives are still a puzzle to them. It will take them some time to put together the pieces. As adults we are still needed, but now in a new way. Standing on the sidelines is not a comfortable position for a parent, a teacher or friend, but do we dare enter the game? We see our teens struggling on the field, and we want to help. The daily question is how?

Teens themselves wonder what we can contribute. Without putting it into words, they constantly challenge us to find our next step in relation to them. For example, they want us to give them more responsibility and trust. But are they ready for these next steps?

Part I of this book is about guiding teens beyond their starting point so they can discover and access the strength of their emerging Self. The starting point is something teens share in common with millions of kids around the world. It is a combination of factors such as family, urban, suburban, or rural environments. It includes their education, their peer experiences, their nationality, and much more. Helping teens see their starting points clearly and guiding them through the key factors in their personality development can help them develop a clear picture of their Self.

To illustrate how the Self emerges in the teen years, we will read excerpts from the diaries of two teens, Carolin and Jason, living in Lackawanna County, Pennsylvania. In these excerpts, they meet the challenges presented by their society, their families, and their own personalities. Carolin has the advantage of a strong and healthy experience of the Self, while Jason has not yet experienced his Self. Jason has not been as fortunate for reasons that become clear as we read about his experiences and see how he grapples with a very reduced power of Self. Both of them are vulnerable, merely by being teens, yet we will see the different ways they respond to the challenges put before them.

In Chapter 3, "The Edge," we explore the differences between "edge experiences" in which the Self engages in the teen's actions and when it does not. It is very important to recognize the difference between these two processes, because the goal with healthy teen activities is to enable the power of the emerging Self to work into the personality. With the importance of this process in mind, adults can focus on the quality of the experiences they create with their teens.

Chapter Four introduces the eight "Key Factors of Personality Development." Because of our individual experiences, each adult places different emphases on the various key factors. And at any given time the teen himself will be working on one or more of these factors. By focusing on these factors we can sharpen our perceptions of the drama the teen is experiencing. These key factors combine all the starting points in a teen's life. What is most exciting is to discover how a teen moves beyond her starting points, for that gives us an idea of how resilient and adaptable the teen will become as she moves into adulthood!

Although teens seldom articulate the Self, they are aware of it, as they experience its growth year after year. What they may talk about are their ideals, the motives for their actions, their relationships with other people, and their changing career goals. Learning to focus and nurture the emerging Self is my goal with Part I of this book.

CHAPTER 1

Carolin

In a passage from her diary Carolin tells her story of being an eighteen-year-old living in Scranton, Pennsylvania. Her parents are divorced, and her mother Karen has been raising two daughters alone for the past four years while teaching fifth grade in West Scranton. Her father Tommy is a successful salesman for the Rigor Corporation. The girls see Tommy only sporadically.

Carolin's sister, Erin, is two years younger. Erin has the advantage of having an older sister who is trying to compensate for a torn-up marriage and two worn out parents. As the older of two children in the family, Carolin carries her sister through the marital conflict the best she can. Like so many first-born children, she is forced to take on too much responsibility at a young age.

Her story begins on the first day of her summer vacation at the shore. As you read her story, try to figure out her underlying attitudes, her relationships, and then identify the quality of Self that shines through her narration. In order to understand the depth of her experiences, may I suggest you try to experience them as intensely as she does in the moment.

Carolin's independent thinking and social initiatives reflect her effort to tap into the core of her personality, that is, whatever makes her essentially Carolin. Her actions are signs of her struggle to connect with her emerging Self.

When I think back on my birthday last spring, I realize my life has changed a lot since then. I just finished my senior year at Scranton High School. I don't give riding lessons any more—too much schoolwork. And I gave up dancing artistically. I miss the charge I get from dancing and, most of all, the way I reveal myself through the movements. Surprisingly enough, Tony and I are still friends even though we are in the process of breaking up. I know it is all over.

Right now I am driving in our car on the way to the shore with my Dad. Every summer he stops at the site where they suppose George Washington crossed the Delaware River to surprise the British. Then he takes our annual detour over to Princeton to buy us some ice cream cones. Pretty weird, if you ask me. He never even went to that college. I can understand the Delaware River site, but the ice cream cones are still a mystery to me. The only connection he has to Princeton is his childhood memories of New York *Giants'* and Philadelphia *Eagles'* exhibition games at the old stadium.

Anyway, glancing out the window my thoughts fly away. I can't stand the radio station we are listening to. Those guys are so neurotic. You would think the world was coming apart at its seams, they make such a big deal out of everything. Get me out of here, please! After a couple of deep breaths and a little mind over matter, I get into the lush landscape in the Delaware River Valley. Trees and hills and fields—greens, hundreds of different shades of green! My favorite colors in the summer!

In my mind I unintentionally talk a little with Tony.

Mr. Garcia, you don't really have to take it so personally. We have to split up because I'm going to college in two months. You are headed to Syracuse and I'm headed to Parsons in New York City. Why did you get so upset last night when I told you it was all over? I've never seen you so lost. Why did you get mad at me?'

My thoughts roll on about as fast as the signs along the highway. We attend our annual stops in memory of the American Revolution and the National Football League and then drive down Route 1 to the Atlantic Ocean!

Around 4:00 in the afternoon we pull into the driveway of my uncle's cottage. The house has been empty for three days, but it is a mess! They must have left in a hurry since there is leftover garbage from a shrimp party. The kitchen stinks like on old fish factory. So Erin and I have the pleasure of cleaning house for the first hour as Tommy, due to his gender, is not very good at such things.

Then we hit the beach without him. The wind is blowing! The Jersey waves roll in. I love the first steps in the sand! At the volleyball net some of my old friends greet us, and we decide to hang out with them. They play seriously. Soon we are ready for the salt water, so we wade out into the afternoon waves and disappear beneath them. Time seems to disappear each time I dive into the ocean. We play around for a while and return to the hot sand. As I lie on the beach towel and let the sun totally penetrate my body, I empty my mind of everything — the shrimp, the radio station, the car ride. I don't hold on to my thoughts about Tony. Not even the mysterious ice cream cone breaks my attention. I relax!

That evening after dinner I had an experience I will never forget! It happened while I rambled down the windswept beach just beyond our uncle's cottage. I walked alone, accompanied only by the green reeds, mixed with some wild-grass that dance to the evening breeze along the dunes. I like the familiar sounds. In the west, a huge red ball of fire is setting just above the tranquil horizon. My eye focuses on its slowly sinking movement. Once again I empty my mind of the daily impressions and let it enjoy five minutes of the disappearing sun. When I stare intensely at the sun, the yellow light radiates into the long flat clouds above, creating white light rims around the clouds. This distracts me. As I look at the purple sky between the clouds and the sun, I wonder whether or not I have ever seen such a color? Just as the great star drops below the horizon, I close my eyes and sink into a peaceful state of mind. Sitting quietly, I reflect inwardly. This second opens up like the curtain on a stage and sends me into a time-span I am not familiar with. At first I'm a little scared but there is no way back. I move into a totally new experience. For how long I cannot tell. When I return to my usual experience of time, I realize, "I am I." The feeling is strangely familiar to me, even though it is new!

Dwelling on the experience for a while, I come to myself but do not open my eyes immediately. It seems like quite a long time, but the feelings are real. And it feels good! Then I open my eyes again. New thoughts cross my mind. I don't feel like the same girl who was sitting in the car today, listening to the neurotic radio station. A realization hits me, "There is much more to the world than I ever thought. I am more than just Carolin as others perceive me and want me to be."

I stand up and brush off the sand. These thoughts accompany me as I walk farther along the sandy beach and let the experience sink in. Yes, it feels good. My eyes look around at the gulls diving into the ocean and the plane cruising high above. I turn my head back to the evening sky still a glow. It amazes me. I keep walking towards the little inlet that I chose not to cross and turn around. What actually happened to me? What has changed? I watch my feet shuffle on the sand. They are mine. I look at my hands and turn them around to see all the movements my hands and fingers can make. It feels like I have gone beyond my body and seen new parts of me. Now that I am back into my usual way of thinking I realize there are unknown parts to all of us. It is so powerful that I chose to be quiet and just let it slowly sink in.

Late the following morning, in the privacy of my bedroom, I am curious about a book by Herman Hesse that I had found on the sandy shelf in my uncle's den. I heard about the book from my friend Sandy who considers herself something of an intellectual. My father opens the door uninvited. He looks a little awkward. Never before have I not shown up for breakfast and hit the beach as soon as I can. He wants to know why I am so distant today — why am I not out on the beach? This is the first time he ever noticed me breaking one of my routines, so I am surprised. I guess he heard that I've stopped dancing and riding and that I haven't felt very strong lately. So rather than telling him what really is going on, I decide to distract him with my physical problems.

What shall I say? I mumbled, "I have a recurring experience. The only way I can describe it is to compare it to a dam. You know when they open the dam to lower the water level of the river — huge, roaring waves burst upon the rocks below. You hear the deep, thunder-like drone of water exploding on the granite as it surges down the river. That is what happens to me. I lose all my energy! Without even knowing it, an opening is made in my energy levels, and all of my energy rushes out. It happens again and again. Then I have to build myself up again. Didn't you tell me once that I had problems walking as a child? Can you tell me more about the first years of my life from a medical point of view?"

He doesn't know what to say: "I was just wondering where you are. I see you are reading my brother's copy of *Steppenwolf*. Don't forget to make your bed." And he was gone.

I didn't tell him, but I know something shifted in me as I watched the sunset last evening on the beach. It is powerful, and I can still feel the moment. There is a lot going on. Even my body feels different. There is no doubt about it—I'm feeling torn in so many directions.

I can go both ways. This is new territory!

In order to distract myself, I open the book again to the page in the first chapter where the narrator allows himself to insert his psychological interpretations of the stranger, Harry Haller. Hesse raises the issue of the stranger being brought up by pious parents and teachers who believe in breaking the will of a teen in order to create a successful upbringing and education. Haller considers this attempt to destroy his personality unsuccessful! The Steppenwolf is too strong and proud for that. Wait a minute. Stop right there. I close the book in outrage! Turning over on my back I look up at the ceiling. Two questions occupy my mind:

Do they really know how to break a kid's will?
How do they destroy someone's personality?

I lay stunned for some minutes. I hate brutality. Brutal people disgust me! Slowly I stand up and walk to the shower. In the bathroom I splash some water on my face, undress, and turn on the cold water in the shower.

When I finish, I return to my room and open the drawers to find a T-shirt for the day. I settle for the *Bruce Springsteen USA Tour* shirt. It is not especially fresh after the winter, but who cares! After slipping on my bikini, I grab a towel, some lotion, my glasses, and the book. Then I walk out on the hot sand.

In her diary Carolin expresses a totally new experience for her. Just after she stares at the light of the huge red ball of fire setting above the horizon, she has an "I am I" experience. She writes that it leaves her feeling "familiar but new!" This is a teen's way of expressing what I call the "edge experience." The "edge experience" takes place when the individual's Self engages in his or her actions. Although she cannot yet articulate it as I do in this book, Carolin has experienced her Self. This breakthrough in her personality development can lead to such essential aspects as: new maturity, more consistency in her actions, personal morality, or productive decision-making abilities.

Carolin's experience on the dunes that evening took place in her heart. She can now make that significant experience an integral part of her daily life by working to develop her own concept of the Self. This process takes time as she learns how to focus on the Self. As her mentor, I will challenge her to further develop her intelligences and her sensory experiences. In Parts II and III you will read how this leads her to healthy personality development in her teenage years and beyond.

But first I will introduce Jason, the other leading character in this book.

CHAPTER 2

Jason

Jason is a teen who is struggling! His daily drama is preventing his Self from emerging, making it much harder for him to get in touch with what is unique about himself and establish relationships with others. In the narration from his diary that follows, notice the direction his life is taking. His defeatist attitude is severe. He drowns in his relationship to his parents, his peers, and his cultural background. Unlike Carolin, he has not experienced his Self.

Jason is at a disadvantage because his parents have no idea about the process of personality development and are in full denial of the Self. Stuck in old habits and bad attitudes, his parents have lost their creativity and their keenness. Jason's father, Alex, is sometimes abusive. Consequently, it is not easy for Jason to develop devotion and respect when his father is so aggressive and out of control. Jason needs a father who will give him the type of affection and affirmation that he deserves. But as you'll read, that is not going to happen. Instead, Jason acts as his parents expect him to—avoiding the issues he needs to address. He plays a role he does not fit.

The bonds to his parents are no longer contributing positive challenges. Since they are not positive role models, he feels unprotected and lonely, and he compares himself to peers, focusing too much on his weaknesses rather than concentrating on his strengths and enjoying life. Notice how he gradually loses contact with his feelings. Without connection, affirmation, and positive reinforcement of what is unique about him, his thoughts become cold and random.

After high school graduation he is even more lost than he was previously. Jason is losing his reverence for himself, his loved ones, and the world at large. This is a very serious condition for him, because he develops a disturbed *Sense of Self* that is unable to prevent many years of destructive experiences.

I keep my eye on the dirt road, as my old black Buick bounces over the bumps as smoothly as a kayak floating over an ocean wave. It just rolls it out. I like the bouncing feeling of the sedan. It is part of my relaxing on the way to the river. This is a familiar part of the woods to which I always enjoy returning. I like to drive out here in the evenings with Cindy. We cruise past the last housing developments, out past the paved roads, out past the road signs, and into the private property territory. What would I do in Clarks Summit without my wheels?

As I write this, I am eighteen years old. Just graduated from Abington Heights High School. They really cared about us. I really like the school, but I got frustrated taking orders and following rules, especially rules that didn't make any sense to me. My English teacher — Freckles — was a jerk. I mean he was a real jerk. I was smarter than him. I figured out how to get a master key to most of the buildings.

This morning I stop the car by the bridge, jump out, and open the trunk. Grasping my fly rod in the aluminum container I slowly unscrew the end to pull out my tempered, seven-foot delight. The early morning Pennsylvania dew is refreshing. As I put the reel on the fly rod, I notice a mosquito sucking into my neck. "Gotchha!" I yell as I feel my blood melt into the palm of my hand.

The light of the early morning sun rising above the hills filters through the heavy forest and starts its morning dance on the surface of the creek. Once the rod is ready, I pull up my waders and ramble down the bank to some boulders lodged into the side of the hill. Jumping up on one, I look at the pool below and decide where to approach the water with my wet fly. I usually start off with a trusty muddler of one kind or another. I tie it and then loft the line to the deepest side of the whirling pool. Once it sinks, I work the fly up towards the bubbling ebb. It takes some time to cover the pool pulling the line rhythmically with my left hand.

I become further distracted when the sensuality of the stream and the woods brings me into an early morning daydream of Cindy. Her touch, the smell of her skin, the way she moves drives my fantasy so far, that I drop the line in the pool long enough to get it stuck on a crag. I have to cross the creek to free the line from an angle. Once it is free, I walk downstream to find a better hole.

My thoughts wander to my sister Laura. She keeps her sense of humor despite our family madness. I tease the daylights out of her! But she handles it gracefully. I don't know when I last heard her get into trouble. She is Mom's delight. Laura and I usually see the situation differently. She reads books. I read the sports page. She does her homework. I put it off. She even cleans her room. Don't ask me why. I am good at putting things into the dishwasher. I can do that all day long, but starting it is another question. And you will never see me taking things out of it!

Laura just got her driver's license. She and her friends are real busy.

Mom is all right. I like her. She really cares about us and gives us her best. For her sake though, I wish she could get more out of life. Routine has taken her over.

We go for walks once and awhile. Those are the only moments in which she opens up to me. It is scary to see how stuck she is. Ten years from now, I bet she will be talking about the same old things.

After a few hours of fishing I drive home and walk into the kitchen looking for some distractions. I open up a can of ginger ale and try to figure which computer games to play for the next half-hour. I have a whole room full of heavy videos and cool play station games. They make the days roll by. Violence and action are cool. I can handle it.

As I open the can, I look out the window and notice a car driving into our driveway. I hear it turning around. While I pour the soda into the tall glass with ice cubes, I look out the window and see that it is Harald. Last week he found the ladder up to this outrageous bridge at Nicholsen. It is the largest aqueduct on the North American continent. They built it for the Erie Lackawanna Railroad at the turn of the Twentieth Century. Today we will cruise up there for some fun.

Since July 3rd I have been working for the bank in Scranton driving in loan payments. My father drops me off on his way to work. I am on the phone every day with people who can't meet their loan payments. I listen to their story and do my detective work. Maybe I can help them solve their problems. It is easy to discover how they are faking it. Sometimes I talk with parents who really have serious problems. Things are falling apart for them. They have lost their job. Others are grieving for lost ones who no longer support them. Shall I get tough with them? Or shall I be understanding and help them restructure their finances? Now I see why this is a summer job for high school grads. Adults don't thrive on taking advantage of people when they are down. There isn't a lot of mercy in this game.

One guy I am working with is interesting. He is smart as hell and good with people. I like the way he speaks with all kinds of customers and genuinely shows them his concern. He makes them comfortable. Mr. Grabowski is always fun to meet. He is real. Too bad that people like him are few and far between!

Two guys in town really bother me. I am working on their unpaid loans. They love themselves and hate anyone in their way. Their narrow look on life makes them petty and hostile. They pretend they are always in control. Such guys are a dime a dozen — the types who always want absolute power over their girls, their friends, and over each and every situation they get into. What a bunch of losers! I stay as far away from them as possible. But I have to make them pay their bills.

After work I usually drive home and relax a bit. There is not much going on. The joy of my life is an old friend who I am dating. Cindy and I hit it off six weeks ago at a picnic, and we haven't stopped talking since. I can't believe how interesting she is! We have known each other for some years, but now we are inseparable.

What really gets me down is my old man. Two nights ago after dinner I knew very well what to expect. Dad was pissed again! At whom? Take an easy guess. Why? I don't know! Life is a big struggle for him. Now he wants me to succeed. So he often gets ugly about things.

"Sit down," Dad said with his familiar sour voice after a couple of drinks.

So I take a seat on the couch. He seizes his glass of whiskey, snatches the paper off the table, flings it open, and says:

"Now look here. I have taught you how to act in a classy and respectful manner, but that is not enough. You want to be on the sports page, you have to be more aggressive! You want to make it in business, you also have to get aggressive. You want to succeed at Penn State, you got to get the most out of it. You really pansy foot at work these days. I know. I have talked with your boss."

I manage to make a stand by saying, "I don't agree with you. When did you speak with him? I work hard enough. You don't need to be super aggressive all the time. Give me a break."

Dad avoids my comments and just walks out of the den. As usual, he refuses to speak with me for the rest of the evening.

Sometimes I wonder if his behavior is for real. His aggression returns regularly, like a nightmare I have had since I was a child. In the dream I see myself running full speed. I run and run and run. Usually, my tormentor unexpectedly creeps up on me, disguised as a massive, ugly feeling that I know very well. I have to run for my life. So I run even faster and start jumping over hills, under fences and through the woods. But the fear just stays right there. I never get far enough away.

I don't play on any baseball teams these days. I don't know. I feel like taking a break. I won't be playing at Penn State so I might as well do something new. The question now is what that will be? I am a jack-of-all-trades and master of none. And I have no idea how I want to make a living for the rest of my life. Not much happening these days. I have nothing to brag about. Every night we usually meet down at O'Niel's and drink some Rolling Rocks. When Nathan is in town, we put down some Tequila and drive home. It is crazy. Not very smart, but hey, that is how we spend our time. I notice it the day after at work. I feel useless. It gives me the emptiness you feel when you walk down burning sidewalks, smelling greasy food, and you have nothing to do. When I get that feeling, I can't concentrate on my customers. I feel dull. It is like who gives a damn! So many phonies walking around in their cool suits talking with cool phrases. You would think they had it together. Big names, big institutions to hide behind. The latest news in their brains — not much more! What is the point? Abuse pays, so don't ask irrelevant questions.

Mark left for California last week. He asked me to take the year off with him, but I am staying right here. He will work for his uncle in Oakland for four months and then meet some friends to travel to Mexico for a month. After Christmas they also plan on heading down to Chile. The mountains, the Inca culture, the language fascinate him. Why learn Spanish in Pennsylvania when you can live with the people? College is not an option for him this year. From Chile those guys want to work on fishing boats to Fiji and New Zealand. They are wild and ready for some adventures!

This morning they called me from the hospital. Cindy is in the intensive care unit. Her vehicle hit a tree after it flipped down a steep gulch off the highway in the Poconos last night. When the paramedics reached the scene, she was still breathing but in very serious condition. All they could tell us was to get there as soon as possible. I visited her briefly this morning, but she is still unconscious. Things do not look good. They think she is fading slowly.

At the age of eighteen Jason is becoming cynical and dull. He is not creating new concepts and meaningful content in his life. The boy drinks too much and thereby creates a larger gap between himself and his emerging Self. Then Cindy's accident takes away the one person with whom Jason has been able to connect, and her loss will also have very detrimental effects on his ability to get in touch with his Self. On the surface Jason is a popular, outgoing guy; on the inside he is not connecting to his most valuable resources. You will read how the gap does not close, and his problems worsen during his freshman year at college.

Before we return to Jason and Carolin in Chapter 5, I want to clarify my concept of personality development in Chapters 3 and 4. This will help you grasp the factors I emphasize when teaching, parenting, or mentoring teens.

CHAPTER 3

The Edge

The "edge experience" is that critical moment in a teenager's life when the Self fully engages his or her actions. In these moments teens discover the unique aspects of their personality. As you will remember from Carolin's story, she had her first conscious "edge experience" on the shore that early summer evening when she realized, "I am I." Since then she has experienced her Self fully engaged in her actions a number of times. Each time her "edge experiences" bring her in tune with her true potential. These experiences are the key to her future because they help her identify what is worth living and working for. The most important aspect of her "edge experiences" is the fact that she gets a glimpse of who she is becoming. Carolin's ability to observe herself "torn in different directions" indicates moral responsibility for her own actions. She identifies her dilemma and does not try to avoid it as Jason chooses to do. It is amazing to speak with teens who receive this confirmation of their identity. They feel acknowledged. Their integrity is strengthened!

Every "edge experience" is an action through which the teen creates her future. Why is this so? The future is created because the teen is able to connect the power of the Self with his or her actions. Put another way, when the Self is present, Carolin's actions are filled with thoughts or feelings that are tempered by values. The power of her true ideals and productive ideas works into her personality as each "edge experience" takes place. For example, Hilde, a teenage activist, told me that her decision to save a wilderness area struck her "like lightening." That phrase indicated to me that she had an "edge experience." Such experiences may last for a brief moment or over a longer period of time. To define and appreciate the "edge experience," Hilde must leave it. In order to get back to it and determine if it has become truly important to her, that is, if it has been incorporated into her personality, she will have to test the reality of her activist plans on a daily basis. Every time, getting to the edge depends on her initiative. She has to want the changes, or they will never happen.

Many kids have the courage to take chances and push through the myriad resistances that put them down and lead them away from their edge. Those resistances can be peers, parents, and experiences that undermine development or institutions that ignore teens' search for vital resources in their personality. Yet I watch teens teach themselves how to connect with their Self and bring it into play in their daily lives. These kids have remarkable presence!

I know teens who are blessed with such powerful "edge experiences" that important steps in their personal growth take place. This growth may take the form of a realization that they want to change important parts of their lives, like working habits, and how they treat other people. They may decide to take risks in their social life that lead to accountability and new confidence. One of my pupils had been a computer geek for five years when he realized that his life was becoming more and more narrow. He left home and worked on a farm for a year, the last thing anyone ever expected him to do! But experiencing the edge gave him new insight into how he wants to live his life.

Another pupil with "edge experiences" learned from his mistakes. Up until the age of seventeen he had been arrogant and at times cruel to his sister. When he saw himself in a moment of "edge experience," he realized he had terrible habits. It didn't take long for him to turn himself around.

Though a teen becomes conscious of his "edge experiences," life does not necessarily get easier. Many become insecure. All of them see more clearly the discrepancy between what is true and false. The fact that they have discovered a part of the potential of their Self leaves them with new gaps. The best way to bridge that gap is to continuously work towards more continuity in decision-making, setting right priorities and unfolding their personal maturity. This is not easy for teens to do alone. They need strong adults to give them guidance along the way. This book will guide you — the parent, teacher, or the friend — in helping you challenge your teen.

For long periods of time teens can become temporarily lost or confused. They may indulge in excessive behavior as a reaction to the superficial world. They have not yet learned how to fill their lives with meaningful content! In some cases their schools and employers stifle their creative vitality. The kids realize that they do not really belong within these institutions. Temporarily, their substantial talents become wasted in a sense of powerlessness. When you see a teen experiencing this kind of confusion, you can bet that his or her Self is not engaged sufficiently.

Carolin is an example of a teenager who continues to have unsettling experiences on the edge. The positive side of her "edge experiences" is that old parts of her personality break away, resurface, and stare her in the face. This process leaves her with decisions to make. For example she knows she has to let go of her parents' problems. They still drain her. When she is drained, her senses shut down, and she loses all energy. The dam opens, and the water rushes out!

How is she putting all this together? First of all, Carolin does not deny what she sees. She acknowledges each experience for what it is worth and then sorts out the impressions. You read about her ability to make decisions in her diary when she explained how she is breaking up with Tony. She reflects about it in the car on the way to the shore.

Because she trusts the power of her Self, she can take the chaos she meets in herself and in others with a sense of humor. She often sees how friends and family drag her into their chaos. During those days she is very vulnerable. Yet Carolin has the advantage of observing that she is in extreme imbalance. She is able to follow her reactions and not drown in the situation. When the experiences are too difficult she works that much harder. This ability helps her step into the future with new strength. She does not use drugs or other means of escaping, because she trusts her ability to push the edge and integrate the experiences during the following weeks. She respects her inner freedom.

In her diary you may have noticed how she handled her father the day after her first conscious "edge experience." She decided not to mention it to him. Carolin felt the "edge experience" was familiar, and she let it continue to influence her without denying it. She noticed it even in her physical body. And the passage from Hesse led her to question, " Do they really know how to break a kid's will?"

This shows the maturity with which she integrates the experience and the solidarity she feels through her vulnerability!

Conventional Experiences on the Edge

Teens hit their conventional edge every day. There they explore the boundaries of their existence. Why do I call it conventional? The conventional edge experiences differ from the "edge experiences" in that we can not be sure that the Self is engaging in the experiences on the edge. It may and it may not. For example, Carolin pushes herself intellectually, often to the point of exhaustion, but it is very difficult for us to know how much of her Self is engaged in the intellectual activity. In nature she tests the limits of her physical prowess, especially when she rides a horse or jumps off a cliff. With her boyfriend Tony she also goes out on the edge. Carolin consistently goes to the conventional edge of her emotional, intellectual and physical resources. There she learns how to continuously push beyond her boundaries, as we noticed in her diary.

As a teacher I have seen kids quickly tap into their intellectual edge during my lessons and ignite the conversation for everyone. They know how to inspire a room of peers by putting their ideas into powerful words or asking the right question! Some of my pupils have an artistic edge. They reach their boundaries as musicians, dancers, or painters and push on to new experiences. What do they bring to their boundaries? They bring their will to be creative, their passion for dramatic experiences. They provoke the edge, incorporate the experience into their Self, and then reap the rewards.

As we can see from his story, Jason is too passive to get out on his edge. He is drowning in his lack of confidence and direction. His parents are still controlling too much of his teenage life, as revealed in his diary by the way his father pushes Jason around emotionally. We also see their control in his use of alcohol. By drinking excessively he prevents a conscious awakening from forming within. If he gets into other areas of substance abuse, he will lose even more contact with his Self. Kids like Jason very often drown in meaningless actions, destructive thoughts, or disconnected feelings because they have not matured. In many cases, they continue this reckless behavior year after year before the adults in their lives see what is really happening.

The emotional edge is explosive for all kids! Their Self is not necessarily engaged in the explosions. Here we see our kids exploring a wide spectrum of experiences. Sometimes they open up to their friends. At other times they hide away emotionally. Quite often they get involved with reckless abandon. The conventional, emotional edge comes from the power of the personality, and it often overwhelms the Self.

For the most part, kids can learn from their experiences through constructive dialogues with other teens or adults. That is preventative medicine, because it takes place over time, and they learn how other people deal with their emotional edge. In the classroom teachers constantly receive distinct impressions of a pupil's emotional edge. A major challenge for teachers—

but also extremely rewarding one — is to figure out how to reinforce those edges in a way that leaves most of the work to the student herself while ensuring that work will be productive. Those of us who are fascinated by human behavior can learn something new every day from the amazing kids we meet and work with.

How Do You Know When Kids are on the Edge?

As I mentioned previously, the most important factor in "edge experiences" is whether or not the Self is engaged in the process. From the sidelines, concerned adults can learn to observe the quality of Self working into their teen`s experiences. This book helps parents and professionals learn to focus on this essential side of teenage personality development. A picture of healthy edge experiences looks like this:

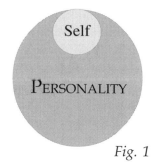

Fig. 1

The Self is the core of the teen's personality. It is present in the personality, and it engages in their actions. In order to observe the core of the personality in our teens, we need to focus our attention on it over a long period of time.

The first clear sign you may notice of a teen experiencing the edge is usually a major change in attitudes, thoughts, or activities. If you notice new ideas they are thinking or a new sense of maturity in the way they address daily issues, these may be signs that the teen's Self is integrating into her personality in a new way. You may also notice that she is dealing with people better.

Notice new self-esteem in the way she presents herself. You may hear your teen express sound insight in an area that you did not expect. These are great moments that tell you that your teen is taking new steps toward newfound maturity, toward discovering the essence of who she is becoming. She's discovering new ideas through "edge experiences." She may not tell anyone, but the ideas are working into her daily life giving her direction and self-confidence. Only some of these signs of "edge experiences" surface well enough for us to see. And talking about them is not always the best thing to do, unless the teen directly asks for recognition or for adult insight.

The insecurity that often arises when teens have "edge experiences" shows that they are struggling for more clarity. They search for a new balance between the old and the new. When old experiences are judged and integrated by the teen's Self, the teen can then appreciate the new experiences. We can see this process very clearly in the changes that take place when teens fall in love. A fifteen-year-old falls in love in a whole different way than a seventeen-year-old or a nineteen-year-old does! The motives for falling in love change between seventeen and nineteen. The depth and the quality of the relationship is also much more advanced. What makes the difference? It is the quality of Self working into their lives through the edge experiences they are going through. In each phase of their lives, new confidence is created.

Nobody is perfect. Teens can always make new moves. And if teens have already made plenty of bad moves, nothing is final. The edge is out there. What is most important is that they repeatedly find their way to healthy "edge experiences." Then they take new steps. A good experience one day may be followed by a bad experience the next day. And a bad experience one day can lead to a good experience the next day. Teenage life is that dramatic. Once again, the key is how much of the Self integrates into the good and difficult experiences. This is essential because the Self — that powerful feeling of being unique — is the teenager's true source of health.

Reach their Attitudes!

Most adolescents are at the mercy of their attitudes. Attitudes lie even more deeply in the personality than the teenager's temperament or feelings. Each attitude has its inherent strengths and weaknesses. How attitudes are dealt with is the real key to self-esteem. If they are used productively, then new sides of life can be unfolded. The power of the Self, available through the "edge experience," gives teens the ability to work productively with their attitudes. Productive attitudes lead to openness and understanding. Unproductive attitudes such as self-pity or " I deserve more" create fear. Fear often leads to extreme self-consciousness or dullness. Eventually these unproductive attitudes lock the teenager into grudges or hate.

We all recognize these attitudes that teens frequently expre

> They do not understand me.
> Things usually never work out for me.
> I never know what to do.
> I always get what I want.

The challenge for adults who care about teens is to help them create a productive relationship with their attitudes. In all my years of teaching and parenting, the toughest job has always been to confront a kid with her unproductive attitude — whether that attitude was egotistical — or based on lack of respect or insecurity! I always had to be sure that my judgment was fair and that my intentions were good. Even then it is never easy to take a stand and enter an unpleasant area with a teen who is in a lot of pain! Once you tell her how you experience her way of behaving, you strike a deep chord in her personality. You have to be direct and aim correctly or you may miss your target — the bad attitude that is slowly destroying a lot of the creativity in her personality. How might this teen respond? Some kids have been so shocked at my approach to them that they simply look at me and acknowledge my insight. These kids are easy to work with because they want to change and they trust me to guide them. One fourteen-year-old boy was not that responsive. He did not like being confronted! Instead of acknowledging that I might have been on to something true, if unpleasant, about him, he just punched me in the face!

Another boy needed a whole year of direct confrontation with clear feedback and a lot of love in order to turn around his destructive attitude about himself. I had to go so far as to recommend that he leave school and get a start somewhere else. In the end he recognized my recommendation as a wake-up call and decided to stay. The turnaround he created inspired the whole class. He gave us all a lot of love.

We are now considering a very critical area of personality development. Many kids are left on their own to make necessary changes. They have unlimited freedom. Along with freedom always comes responsibility that they are sometimes too inexperienced to handle. Without responsibility, though, kids will not lead productive lives. Those who have not learned to be responsible for themselves and others often receive brutal messages from their peers or adults who exploit their weakness. Such responses would not be necessary if adults who truly care about them had been able, in a loving way, to help them turn around their bad attitudes.

Identify their Multiple Attitudes

If you look deeply into your kid's attitudes, you will be surprised how complicated and potentially explosive their situation really is. Some teenagers combine superficial attitudes with arrogance and often have a hard time learning from their own mistakes. These teens then often have an experience of fate striking them hard blows that seem to come out of nowhere! With "out of nowhere" I mean blows that are unexpected. They are dealt by strangers who respond to the teen's attitudes mercilessly. I often tell parents that if they don't take it upon themselves to teach their kids what is fair and respectful, other people will deal their kids unpleasant and maybe even tragic blows from outside the family. Such hard blows seem to come out of nowhere but really come from the teen's inability to excise their bad attitudes from their moral Selves.

One of my pupils had a superficial attitude that reinforced her fatalistic attitudes. She had struggled for years to keep her balance between vulnerability and durability. She chose to be superficial about her experiences, always covering up her lack of confidence with arrogant comments about other teens. Christine did not believe in herself, and her self-esteem dwindled year after year. She became a master at pulling herself together to hide her pain and perform well. Unfortunately, she built up so much denial that she also became a master at avoiding personal issues.

Kids often need help from trustworthy adults to identify their own attitudes. It is hard to put your finger on deeply anchored problems, and when you do, you must expect extreme resistance! If you dare to tell a seventeen-year-old that he has an extremely positive attitude of carrying on despite resistance, he will be very happy. If you dare to tell an eighteen-year-old such as Jason that he is wasting a lot of his time and energy with his fatalistic attitude, and point out examples of what you mean, he may not appreciate it at the moment, but there is a good chance he will years later. As I noted above, it is up to the teenager to take responsibility for any changes he may find necessary.

Bad Attitudes below the Edge

When teens have multiple bad attitudes, there is great potential for conflict. They dwell in experiences far below the edge that put them in a self-destructive zone where they easily make life miserable for themselves and others.

For example, the wise guys who seek immediate gratification may be frustrated by not getting what they think they deserve. They express negative attitudes such as:

I want it and I want it now.
I have it all but I deserve more.
They sold me short.

Quite often these teens combine their bad attitudes with another devastating one: placing the blame on others! The problem is them—not me! These teens take this attitude to another level by stating, "Either you are for us or you are against us!"

A fourth bad attitude that may complicate the picture is: "I won't make an effort to change, and I don't have to explain anything to anybody!"

If teens indulge in more than one negative attitude, they find it extremely hard to make significant changes. Such teens risk becoming lean young wolves with bad attitudes continually scorning others in their spiral of hate. Grudges and total lack of understanding for other ways of life build up. The personality development of such extreme teens with multiple bad attitudes is limited unless an adult is there to prevent a loss of Self.

A Loss of Self

What is happening psychologically when teens turn to violence? What makes a teen say to another person, " *I hate you!*" What type of personality are we dealing with when a teen calls in a bomb threat to a high school just for fun? What is missing when teens commit well-thought-out crimes or become premeditated murderers? Such teens, suffering from twisted minds and bizarre behavior, carry an aura of invincibility. They believe they can live way beyond the law.

The Columbine High School Massacre on April 20, 1999, in Littleton, Colorado, is an example of the tragedy of denying the Self. The kids who stormed into the school with semiautomatic weapons and explosives were filled with hate, not the power of the Self. What made them laugh as they shot their fellow students hiding under the tables? How could they shoot at propane-tank bombs they planted around the school and then amuse themselves by trying to pick off teachers running through the hallway? How could they kill 12 students and a teacher while injuring 23 other kids before turning their weapons on themselves?

They were filled with hate because they had no sense of belonging—and no one they could look up to. They lacked the power of their Self and instead responded with the power of hate. The following picture of hate took possession of their personality.

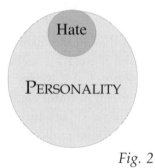

Fig. 2

A tragically destructive circle of hate can eventually take the place of the Self in the teenage personality. In these cases, the Self did not work into their daily life or take part in their actions. Nor did it inspire their thoughts with good ideas and healthy ideals. Whenever the teen does not connect with the Self, destruction fills the gap. This extreme situation is now a national problem. Too many kids are living without productive "edge experiences."

Teens at severe risk do not connect with anyone. They start forcing their attitudes on others. In this way they unconsciously affect the willpower of other kids. I have seen kids in this phase take pleasure in tormenting animals on field trips. Often they continue the amusement in the classroom by tormenting other kids and abusing any teacher who lets them. Parents who observe these symptoms at home and teachers who see it at school need to react appropriately each time they appear. Chapters 6,

7, 10 and 11 of this book will give you the keys to actions you can take to prevent your kids from developing the power of hate.

There are three phases in the process by which teens either lose contact with the Self or never develop a healthy relationship with it.

The first phase starts when teens consciously use their power to affect the will of others — that is, they no longer have any genuine interest in other people. They merely enjoy using people! These teens are mean and egotistical. Some of them are in contact with adults who teach them the power of hate. We define this power as purely egotistical love that is always at the expense of others! Such adults lead kids down a dark path of destruction.

The second phase starts when the teen develops his hate on a daily basis and learns how to systematically manipulate others. He gets other kids to work for him. He uses violent videos, computer games, drugs, and alcohol to build up his rage. These crutches help him lose the control that would otherwise put the brakes on such activities. Daily dosages of second-hand violence make him feel good. His fantasy life dwells on abuse. He learns how to bring hate into his personality, thereby displacing the good, moral impulses of the Self.

These attitudes continue into the third phase, where he decides to kill. I have never worked with kids in this phase. The symptoms in the first and second phases are clear enough for any caring adult to identify. The third phase is more difficult, because the teen has placed his intelligence in the service of pure hate and uses that intelligence to prevent others from identifying him. He may collect weapons and learn how to use them in his plans to ruin the lives of as many people as possible.

The temptations of hate are always present if teens do not get in touch with their Self. "Edge experiences" are important because they reinforce a teen's growing perceptions of truth and love, especially when the Self is engaged in the activity. Conventional experiences on the edge are more common and of no less importance. Just how well we can support our kids on the teenage edge depends on our focus and efforts.

With the significance of "edge experiences" in mind, we move forward to the next chapter where we will look at eight key factors of personality development. We will focus on each one of these factors and explore how the Self gradually emerges during the teenage years.

CHAPTER 4

The Key Factors of Personality Development

As I write this chapter, I am down in the basement, out of bounds. The roof is bouncing up and down to the beat of the high school kids partying the night before they graduate. I hear such lyrics as:

> Tell me what you like baby! Tell me what you want!
> How do I breathe without you?
> I'm never gonna be the same. . . .

They celebrate three years of friendship. It is the last night they will all be together. Tomorrow they each go in their own directions. Will they ever cross each other's path again? One thing is for sure — they are enjoying putting high school behind them!

Hopefully, these kids will be fine. Not perfect but vulnerable. Not passive but creative. Not stupid but curious! A big part of their success in life will be their ability to work with all eight of the key factors in their personalities. Will their Self emerge powerfully enough to integrate important sides of their personalities? Will their *Sense of Self* be healthy and productive? These are the questions concerned adults should work with daily.

Depending on their approach to teen development, experts will disagree about what constitutes the key factors of personal ity development. Diverse approaches are natural, given the complexity of the subject. I see eight key factors in teenage personality development.

The Eight Key Factors of Personality Development

   1. The Self
   2. Personality as of this Moment
   3. The Cognitive Profile
   4. Cultural Background and Gender
   5. Parents
   6. Schooling
   7. Peer Conditioning
   8. Genes and Experience

Trying to understand the key factors in teenage self-development is always complicated. All eight factors play an intricate role in the life of a teen. The goal is to decide which factors are most relevant for the moment. Once you make a decision and work on certain factors, new combinations of the eight factors will need to be attended to. Changes occur quickly, and each teenage personality is a complicated being.

The "Edge Theory" in this book addresses the Self, the Sense of Self, and the Cognitive Profile in the teenage years. This theory supplements the decisive work done by many experts in genetics, peer conditioning, schooling, parental influences, cultural background, and gender.

The Self is often left out of professional discussions and daily care by parents. In my opinion personality development comes down to a choice between ignoring the Self or paying attention to it. The Self engages in the personality but is often overshadowed by the immediate power of the personality. When teens tap into the power of the Self, it enhances their access to the other key factors. Because the characteristics of the Self are hard to identify and discuss, most educators and psychiatrists prefer to concentrate on genes, instincts, or intelligence. Often you only hear about the Self in a negative context as the egotistical, selfish, root of suffering.

1. The Self

What exactly does the Self do? As the core of the personality, it presents the personality. The Self makes decisions, defines our priorities, and provides continuity in our existence. It stores our memories. It experiences the world through our senses and interprets our experiences of music. It creates actions based on the motives we have chosen, and much, much more. It is the part of our personality with which we make changes in our lives. In times of illness and crisis, the Self can be especially powerful. With it we can learn from sickness and hardship, and we can grow through incredibly difficult life situations.

Because it is only emerging during adolescence and has not yet fully developed, the Self is more complicated in the teenage years than later on in life. For example, the Self is not yet fully integrated in the key factors of personality development as I mentioned above. That is why teens need young adults and elders who have taken their Self seriously and worked to free it from influences such as the egotism of their personality and unproductive attitudes.

The Self has a coworker — the Sense of Self. This is the sense we use to observe our own actions as well as the Self of others. You will find it explained in detail in Chapter 13. When caring adults work to overcome their egotism and their negative attitudes, they increase the possibility for using their Sense of Self to experience what is really developing in their teen's personality. If adults gain continuity in their Sense of Self, they can in turn guide their teens to a more healthy Sense of Self. Here learning by example works most powerfully and not a lot of talk.

Teens need adults in their lives who recognize what is good, but they also need to break away from their parents and other authorities to bring out the full power in their Self. Otherwise, they suffocate in their past experiences and lack the power to further develop their personality.

Many adults are resistant to the idea of the Self when they first hear about it. I speak with some who actually deny the Self. So before adults see the Self in others, they have to create their own conceptual relationship to it. When that work is well under way, they are better able to recognize and then guide the emergence of the Self in their teen. That is an exciting task!

2. The Personality Factor as of Today

What do we really mean when we talk about the personality? Usually the personality is considered the totality of all personal traits or specific characteristics of a person. In modern psychiatry, the personality is often described as the unique expression of a person's thinking, feeling, and willing. Consistent attributes such as needs, temperament, habits, values, self-image, and behavior also belong to the concept of personality.

All of the above-named areas of personality are in continual change in the teenage years. The teen's personality as it is expressed in the moment provides the foundation for further steps — therefore, I include it as one of the key factors in personality development.

Identity evolves when the teen defines her own reality. It is her way of acknowledging herself in her consciousness. At the same time, she realizes that she exists in other people's consciousness. Identity projects who she thinks she is. Or who she wants to convince herself she is. Her identity also defines what she can do and not do. But identity also gives her a sense of being part of a group: language, family, ethnic community, gender and social norms.

A teen's identity is her daily self. It reflects her lifestyle. It has to do with her perception of her body. It is reflected in her make-up and her wardrobe. She expresses it with her posses-sions, her desires, her daily problems, and much more. Her iden-tity is the central factor in her self-image. The goal for each teen-ager is to develop a true picture of herself that she can accept, and then learn how to lead her life according to that self-image.

When a teenager is not able to retain her lifestyle or self-image, an identity crisis arises. In a time of crisis, it is harder for the teenager to bring her thinking into a healthy relationship with her actions. She is overpowered by a chain of unrelated actions and powerful emotions. Knowing that she knows what she is doing becomes very difficult. And knowing what she is feeling becomes even more difficult. Rather than healthy self-consciousness, a pseudo-self comes into play. Her life interests are then less accessible, and she may take off on a long journey with many detours.

Getting to know their personality in the teenage years dur-ing a time of rapid change is only one aspect of teenage person-ality development. The other aspect is the challenge of coming to terms with the influences of the times, their culture, their he-redity, and the education they receive, and still find an identity that brings them into a healthy relationship with themselves.

In this book I use the term "personality" to express not only a teen's personality, but also his or her identity and daily self. To simplify this definition, I have decided to incorporate all three concepts — identity, daily self, and personality — under the term "personality."

3. The Cognitive Profile

Every teen has unused potential for experiencing the world. This potential is made up of her talents, her personal attributes, and a wide variety of other faculties that are at her disposal. With their cognitive profile teens solve problems they face while they develop new questions. I include two huge areas within the idea of the cognitive profile: eight intelligences and fifteen senses.

A teen can further develop her personality by using the power of her Self to experience new areas of intelligence and sensory perception. The extent to which her cognitive profile is developed will influence her personality development throughout her lifetime. Her profile is defined by the degree to which she is tapping into these faculties, which in turn depends on her attitudes. Positive attitudes open her intelligence and senses to the outside world. She engages. She explores. She reflects. Egotistical attitudes narrow her vision. For example, her attitude may be, "What is in it for me?" Her vision is narrowed by personal gains, security, or power.

To which purpose will she use her intelligences? There is a double-edged sword in the growth of the teenage intellect. Her intelligence can be used for egotistical disdain and hypercritical evaluation of the surrounding environment. Or it may be developed from within her convictions and become the strength of unbiased observation and true interest in the world.

It is extremely valuable for teens to be challenged as to how they will develop their intelligence far into the future. Will she become an egocentric thinker who is especially good at analyzing others? Or will she become a master of operational thought with a limited perspective on the mysteries of life? Will she choose to avoid abstract, analytical thinking in order to develop her artistic abilities? Or will her strength be in mental toughness? For some teens their abundance of chaotic thoughts produces scrambled mental images and a distorted experience of reality. But they also may become clear and flexible thinkers with a moral foundation for their actions. In any case, abstract and logical thinking needs to be developed within their cognitive profile.

In this book I develop the idea of the cognitive profile using two different models. The first is created by Howard Gardner, a psychologist at the Harvard School of Education, who developed a framework for understanding intelligences and talents that he refers to as "multiple intelligences" (1993).[1] He is convinced that adults need to help children develop their natural competencies and gifts by challenging them to go beyond the limiting factor of IQ.

Gardner identifies eight intelligences. The first two are *linguistic* and *logical-mathematical* intelligences, both of which have been put on a pedestal in our society. Then he mentions *spatial* intelligence—a gift that sculptors, sailors, and surgeons have. Musicians and listeners develop *musical intelligence.* *Bodily kinesthetic* intelligence is highly developed by athletes and craftsmen. He also defines two forms of personal intelligence: *interpersonal* and *intrapersonal. Interpersonal* intelligence is used in one's social and professional life, while the *intrapersonal* intelligence is used inward in our own mind. In his book from 1999, *Intelligence Reframed,* Gardner introduces the possibility of three additional intelligences (naturalist, existential and spiritual but adds the *naturalist* as the eighth intelligence of his Multiple Intelligence Theory).

In this book I use the image of the water lily to represent the teenager's personality development. I picture the key factors as the roots of the lily. During the teenage years the Self emerges to become the crown of the lily. Within the crown, the teenage Self accesses the cognitive profile. From a bird's eye view, this image of teenage personality development gives us the crown of the lily containing all eight intelligences as represented in Figure 3 below.

All eight intelligences intermingle in the teen's personality. At any given time she will access a combination of her intelligences within her activities. The power of the Self engages during "edge experiences" to intensify the activity, and her *Sense of Self* enables her to learn from it. Adolescents can focus on developing new intelligences according to their interests.

The other framework is presented by Sir John Eccles in his 1989 book, *Evolution of the Brain: Creation of the Self.*[2] There he describes eight outer senses and seven inner senses. Below, the lily blossom illustrates the outer senses within the cognitive profile:

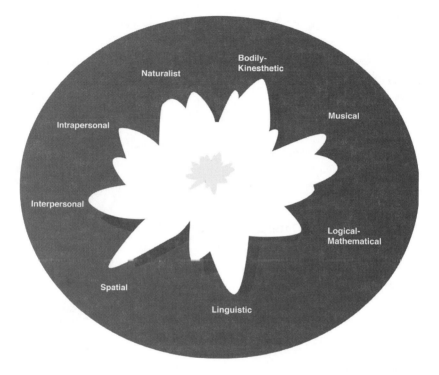

Fig. 3

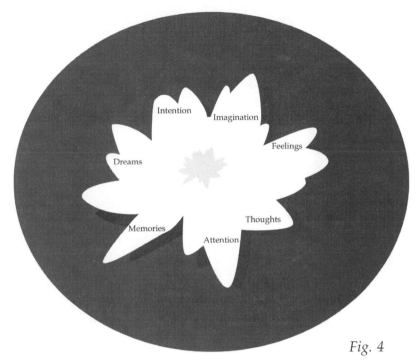

Fig. 4

Teens discover the difference between their inner and outer senses when they engage themselves in sensory activities. Outer senses such as smell, sight, and touch are more common and less individual in the quality of experience. The seven inner senses, on the other hand, require a more active use of the self-conscious mind. They are first accessible to teens coincidentally. Unfortunately, many adults slam the door to their teen's inner senses by telling them what is real or fake and not giving them a chance to figure it out on their own. Many adults have chosen to ignore their own imaginations and fear any new steps into their seven inner senses. But the senses have unlimited potential! Teens are strong enough to tap into the vast experiences of their inner senses. It takes consistent effort.

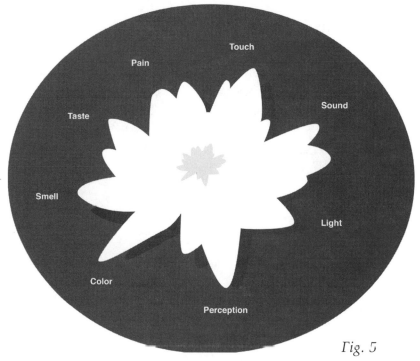

Fig. 5

Sensory experiences and multiple intelligences give us a broad picture of each teen's cognitive profile. They are abilities through which teens experience the world and themselves. The fact that teens can use these abilities as part of their personality development is not new and revolutionary. But each one of these abilities can be the source of a better life when teens grasp them consciously and engage their Self in the process. For some teens, engaging the Self may be a simple thing like hunting, playing basketball, and playing music, or whatever broadens their horizons. It is also extremely interesting for teens to observe how their peers take new steps by using the power of their Self to develop something new in their lives. Suddenly, they start reading a lot or they start dancing a lot. Some learn how to meditate, while others learn how to climb on glaciers. You name it. The opportunities within the cognitive profile are limitless.

A teen takes a major step in her development when she focuses on her Self and uses her cognitive profile to develop new skills in her personality.

4. Schooling

Where else do we spend more time in the teenage years than at school? At school we teach our kids what to think and how to perform. Today, basically two hot areas of activity are rewarded: sports and academics. Other softer or more practical areas in life are tolerated and even respected at certain schools but on a national scale they are considered secondary.

Students like Jason and Carolin are measured nationally only by their academic and athletic performance. The national ratings reward those who do well on SATs, with their grades or in sport events. This standardization of teenage activity creates a very narrow bottleneck that all teens have to navigate as they manage their high school career every day. But according to the Edge Theory, there are many other kinds of intelligence and senses at work, and each one needs to be addressed and developed.

Where do students with strengths beyond academics and sports fit in? For example, Jason is considered a winner on the baseball diamond and on the football field. In the classroom and in his social life he is considered a loser. Carolin is a winner in the classroom but not so in school sports. Socially, she has the advantage of her independent character. She is not popular like some others, but her peers respect her because she respects herself. Carolin is not in the student government and is not a cheerleader, even though one of her best friends is. Two of her friends are well-respected actors. Most of these teens think they have already made it, if for only a temporary period in their lives. Jason, on the other hand, enjoys that special role reserved for jocks. Off the field, he is too emotional to be one of the social elite. As you read in his diary, Jason is very good at entertaining himself, but he is not assertive enough to break into a productive social environment. Instead, he hangs out at the bar with his friends.

Many adolescents like Jason and Carolin do not experience their teen years as a frame in which their creative abilities are fostered and rewarded. Many components of their cognitive profile are temporarily on hold. The definition of winners and losers in our nation's schools is dangerously narrow. How many schools address the teen's Self in its many aspects? My experience has shown that the breadth of the teen's cognitive profile is seldom acknowledged or developed.

5. Cultural and Gender Factors

Jason and Carolin are forming their identities. They try out new styles, new friends, and new ideas, and are greatly influenced by kids around the world. As with everyone else, personality development has been influenced by global standardization. Global tribes have rapidly replaced local customs. For example, kids in Stockholm are Chicago *Bulls* fans. Kids in London belong to the "Friends" tribe! All over the world kids are blasted with global tribal information anyhow, anywhere, and anytime! Instincts are deregulated. Cultural barriers are gradually giving way to commercial interests. Teen culture is massive and getting bigger. When the motive is to sell products to millions of teens by providing an identity based on a brand, the global mentality develops a false sense of identity in teens! The other side of the coin is a productive global mentality in which teens express their true concern for other people's welfare.

Despite our mass culture, teens cannot avoid the basic human need for designing their own lives, which means they must discover their individual values and act responsibly. This process, however, is made more complicated by the powerful influences of global, tribal mentality. As we have seen, our culture rewards winners and ignores losers, making adolescence an extremely vulnerable period. Many experts are convinced that teens derive false and true selves from their cultural influences. Globalization of culture forces teens to abandon their true selves and take up false selves by dictating what the teen values, even if those values do not relate to his world.

The Gender Factor can limit teens as they develop their personality. It is incumbent upon girls to be feminine, so in some cases they relinquish their true selves to that false self in order to conform to peer or parental influences. Boys feel the same pressures. They often must establish a false self to meet the expectations of their culture's role for them. Boys and girls experience their identities as split into serious contradictions. Signs that indicate teens are burdened by a false Sense of Self include the anger, depression, conformity, and withdrawal that we see in so many of them.

6. The Parental Factor

In most cases, parents provide teens with shelter and money. They also give teens protection and support. Just how do parents affect their teens? Whether a parent goes beyond the basics and provides a role model teens want to copy or one that teens want to run from depends on the strength of the parent's Self and how attuned that parent is to the emergence of the Self in their teen. If the parents' relationship to their Self is weak, they easily revert to manipulation in order to maintain control of the parenting process, making it difficult for the teen to create a more mature relationship with that parent. Stern, patronizing parents who reprimand again and again are just as hard to handle as those who ignore or give in to their teens. In both cases the parent is not in touch with the Self's power over their own personality and cannot possibly help his/her teen during these difficult years of transition.

All children grow beyond their childhood roles during the teenage years. The parental-child role also changes dramatically as the teen progresses through the individuation process. You can see this clearly when your fourteen-year-old starts telling you how stupid your comments are, how predictable your be-havior is, and how easy you are to tease. Although teens are becoming independent people, they need their parents more than ever. But their relationship with their parents has to change in order for it to remain a positive one. Teens are searching for their Self, and they need the mature guidance of their parents who are in touch with their own true Selves.

7. The Peer Factor

When teens turn each other on to new sides of life, the per-sonality can be powerfully developed. Girlfriends and boyfriends can really help a kid cut loose and start tapping into her resources. That is one main reason why friends we make in our teen years are some of the most important we make in life!

Peer groups are an inevitable and necessary part of adoles-cent development. They help the teen explore her identity, and they give her an area of competence. She feels connected. Even cliques can be beneficial as long as she does not get stuck in them. They can give her a place to work from that includes recogni-tion and togetherness. A major drawback of peer groups is the pressure to conform to the group's values. In this instance, a member might begin to repress certain aspects of her personal-ity development if she thinks the group won't value these as-pects. Peer groups can become tyrannical and corrosive in this regard. In order to resist that kind of peer pressure, the teen must develop her concept of Self so that she can detect when she is benefiting from association with her peer group or when she is not.

8. The Genetic and Experience Factor

Is all of the personality in the genes? Are all of our memo-ries, our hopes, emotions, talents, and ideas contained in the brain? Some experts are convinced that whenever we speak, scratch an itch, sneeze, or glance up in surprise at some inter-ruption, the impulse to do so originates in the brain. The theory behind this key factor of personality development states that life evolves through random mutations in living things, on which natural selection then acts to promote the survival of the fittest. We are considered survival machines blindly programmed by selfish genes.

With this conviction in mind, many experts choose to ignore the Self by stating that the entire personality and identity are contained in the brain. The goal is to pull the right control levers in our teens' brains in order to make them behave better. The logical conclusion for those who ignore the Self is that teenage behavior is the result of a dialogue between the teen's brain and his experiences. I disagree.

In this book, I will argue that behavior is the result of a dialogue between the teen's Self and his experiences. The genetically based theory inspires teens to work with their brain as the center of their being. My Edge Theory inspires them to work with their Self as the center of their being.

Scientists have discovered that at birth each child has approximately 100 billion neurons that form in the brain more than 50 trillion connections called synapses. They believe that half of the 80,000 different genes a child has are involved in forming and running the central nervous system. Discoveries show that in the first few months of life another factor appears in the motor cortex of the brain—20 times as many synapses have been created in a process called synaptogenesis, creating a total of more than 1000 trillion synapses. Scientists believe these synapses form through experience. There are not enough genes to create such development. Once the new synapses are created, they need to be supported by repeated stimulation. Otherwise, they get pruned away like branches from a tree. In other words, repeated experiences also contribute to the process of synaptogenesis.

The process of synaptogenesis is more commonly known as the "nature-nurture controversy." With nature, many scientists mean "genes," and with nurture they mean "experiences." Both camps will continue to disagree as to which is more important. But it is interesting that they now accept the importance of childhood experiences in the formation of the brain.

Now we have briefly outlined the eight key factors of teenage personality development. All of them are huge. They help adults and teens focus on the factors that are relevant in the moment. There is no universally "right" approach. It is most important that our teens use their key factors to create their future.

Chapter 5

Beyond the Starting Point

This book is about growing beyond the starting point. The starting point is an individual's unique combination of the key factors of personality development that were discussed in Chapter 4. There are as many starting points as there are teens in the world. Regardless of where they live, who their parents are, and how hard a childhood they may have experienced, teens have the ability to create a new and better life and, in fact, need to hurdle themselves beyond their starting points. How successfully they develop beyond their starting points determines much of the happiness they will find in their lives.

All first-hand experiences are the most immediate starting points teens can work with. In this chapter I will show you how I identify which key factors I choose to work with when challenging teens to move beyond their given situations. I will use Carolin and Jason to illustrate strategies for two very different teens. The first step is to identify which key factor of their personality needs attention for whatever reason. The next step is to build a short-term (one week) and a long-term (six months) strategy to develop that aspect of the teen's personality.

Strategy is valuable because it gives the adult a clear picture of what he or she wants to accomplish with the teen. Having a strong picture of how you want to help your teen grow is essential, because it gives you a solid connection to your teen, and it also inspires you in your daily activities. I have met many parents who forget about their children for long periods of time and, therefore, do not give the children the healthy challenges and guidance they truly deserve. These strategies also help the adult pendulate or "breathe" with the relationship, by which I mean engage with your teen, then pull back completely, so the teen can take his or her own steps. If the adult has a good strategy but does not pull back, the teen will feel controlled. If the adult does not get involved, the teen will feel left out. The image of breathing in and out applies to any healthy teen-adult relationship. Let's look at Carolin's starting point and then develop two strategies.

How is Carolin doing at this particular moment?

In rereading Carolin's diary in Chapter 1, my first general conclusion is that she is doing well. I trust she will pull through and lead the life she wants to lead. I draw this conclusion based on two observations: she has the advantage of a supportive mother, and she has her own experiences of her Self as she mentioned on the beach one evening.

Carolin knows where she stands with her parents, but the relationship with her father is still pulling her down. Her physical problems are expressed by a regular loss of energy. Her bouts with stress and lack of energy send her emotional life up and down. To some degree, she sees herself going through these physical setbacks. In addition she is struggling with the vast discrepancy between the world she experiences in her everyday life and the power of her Self. Carolin senses she is in a vulnerable situation, so she decides to avoid explicit violence on TV or in the movies. Even the newspaper doesn't seem to engage her. She dreams of living in Greenwich Village, where she will meet new people.

This girl has clearly become too much for her father to handle, now that she is able to read him so well. She has an uncanny way of knowing what he will say. When they are talking together, Carolin has learned how to avoid subjects she doesn't want to discuss. As a result, Tommy seldom feels he has any room to say anything encouraging to her. It is clear, though, that he does not feel the same affection toward her as he did when she was his little girl. It is a paradox that a man who lacks this maturity has such a unique daughter.

Carolin is very gifted at school, but she reacts to stress by working too hard. She did not set healthy boundaries on her schoolwork. At the end of the school year she worked extremely hard and lost her balance again. This drained her. Her low energy level has become a chronic problem no matter how hard she tries to change. She had these problems since she was a child. Her health is fragile right now.

Luckily, Carolin and her mother Karen have each other. They are open and vulnerable with each other. Both of them are willing to admit mistakes. Karen shows great respect for her daughter's opinion. She considers Carolin a strong individual and is honored to be her mother. Their relationship helps Karen deal with the daily struggles of supporting two girls alone. At times Carolin changes roles with her mother, taking on parental responsibility, for instance, when she helps her mother stop smoking and supports her looking for a new job.

Her natural ability to think for herself gives Carolin a radical edge most people do not notice in her. She is tough and determined. Unlike many other kids her age, she perceives the world wisely. Carolin has lots of problems, but she is not self-destructive. She is living on the edge, and she knows it. The experience of her Self while walking down the beach expanded her horizon significantly. Now she knows that she is not limited to the world of her five senses, that she has an existence beyond her physical body, and that her Self is much more than her daily identity. This experience can become a powerful source of strength for her if she takes it seriously, that is, if she integrates it into her personality. If she does not, such an experience can knock her off balance. Kids who do not integrate their insights of their Self well enough often become disillusioned and arrogant. A more introverted person like Carolin risks becoming extremely self-critical. Integrating her newly found Self is a long-term endeavor, probably lasting her whole life, but she knows she needs to take some new steps this week. As her mentor with full knowledge of her "edge experience," I choose a **short-term strategy** with three of her key factors:

Her Self

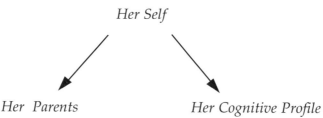

Her Parents   *Her Cognitive Profile*

Whenever I get the opportunity to be a mentor to a teen, my goal is to create a trusting dialogue during the first week. I like to go for a walk with him or her to break the ice and find some common ground. When we talk, I always try to gain their confidence and trust by focusing on my respect for their integrity. This is the approach I take when I speak with Carolin. The best way to get her attention is to mention topics she cares about. Once we have begun to talk, I ask her questions that lead her to tell me more about what is really going on.

Carolin talks with me directly about her experience on the sand dunes. She is unique in her ability to put her experiences into words. I have met very few teens who are as articulate as she is. I listen and help her define her own experience without interpreting it. I realize that the key is to help her take her maturity seriously. This week it would be good for her to identify her Self well enough to feel when it is present in her activities or not! When it is not active in her actions, she is usually overwhelmed by her feelings or chaotic activities.

One way for Carolin to start observing her Self on a more regular basis is to notice the difference in her personality every morning when she wakes up! Every morning the Self comes into the personality and the body. In our talk I challenge Carolin to observe herself waking up in the morning and then grasp the moment when the Self comes fully into her personality. That is the moment she feels awake, refreshed, and full of energy. Some teens experience the Self ten minutes after waking. For others it may take one and a half hours.

I know teens who experience the Self at the start of a new day when they first meet other people. Greeting other people wakes them up. They also awaken to their own Self in such moments. Their *Sense of Self* gives them the experience of their own actions and of the Self of others. This daily experience is as common as drinking water and eating breakfast.

Whenever I guide teens toward an understanding of their personality, I always start with the ability to think. I approach thinking as an intrapersonal intelligence providing the source of inner freedom. I believe Carolin's potential for inner freedom — the ability to determine her own actions, to think her own thoughts, and understand her own feelings — needs to be worked on this week. Her striving for inner freedom will give her more confidence and a good attitude for any work she does.

It is always important for adults to acknowledge in teens some strength that they already possess. In her excerpt, Carolin demonstrated that she is trying to put her relationship with her parents in its right place. Perhaps you remember from her story that she sat in the car daydreaming and began a little talk with her old boyfriend, Tony Garcia. She wondered why he got so upset with her, after all it was all over between them! This shows that she uses her *Sense of Self* to reflect over her actions. She tries to work through her mental images and sort them out. This is a great strength that a mentor should acknowledge and encourage her to develop further. Whenever I notice a teen using her *Sense of self* in a healthy way, I support it as much as possible. I also encourage her to take care of herself and feel good about letting her parents and her little sister lead their lives without her constant attention.

A great way for kids to overcome difficult experiences from their past is to practice using new parts of their cognitive profile. The best contribution I can make is to encourage her to tap into unused aspects of her cognitive abilities. I start with her experiences of nature, including the fact that she experienced her Self on the beach and, thus, has a deep relationship with nature.

An indirect approach is usually wise when talking with teens. I choose one of my experiences in the ocean when I was pulled out to sea after a football practice on Aquidneck Island. To this day, I still don't know why I put myself into that dangerous situation. Nor do I know how I got out of it! I was exhausted after an afternoon training session and jumped into the ocean to cool off. Before I knew it I was being pulled out faster than I realized. To survive I had to swim for thirty minutes as fast as I could even though I was exhausted from the football training.

When I tell her the story, associations arise in her mind, and she naturally relates my story to similar events she has experienced. In no time flat, objective topics such as survival instincts and mind over matter take over our conversation. I paint a picture of a whole spectrum of cognitive possibilities that I had in that dangerous moment off Second Beach. Then I leave it up to her to judge which possibility really mattered. We can talk about cognitive abilities such as attention, memory, and thinking clearly in a dangerous situation. What really happened to me out there? This indirect approach to a serious topic is a good start because I avoid moralizing or being too direct by using myself as the object. At the same time, I am introducing her to her own cognitive potential. The picture of being drawn out to sea is not upsetting to her; she relates to it as a critical edge experience. I challenge her to consider what she would have done. How would she have reacted? If you are able to create a constructive dialogue during the first week, you are off to a good start.

If Carolin does not get in touch with more of her inner freedom and break out of the family experiences that are pulling her down, she will have a hard time accessing her cognitive profile and creating more maturity. Her parents' problems and her bad habits of stress may continue to drain all her energy.

I see three key factors in my **long-term strategy** for Carolin during the next six months.

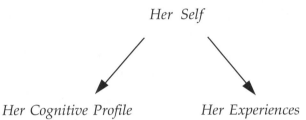

Her Self

Her Cognitive Profile   *Her Experiences*

Because she has already discovered that she has a Self, Carolin is in a different situation from many teens. The great advantage with Carolin is that she is searching! As part of my long-term strategy, I will continue to teach her how to tap into new areas of her cognitive profile. Carolin can use her intrapersonal intelligence to further unfold her inner and outer senses. The key is that she use her intelligences to bring the power of her Self into her senses.

In our talks I challenge Carolin to deepen her experience of nature by using her senses more consciously. In that way she can reach much more depth of experience. Once again, all I can do is mention how to practice developing her cognitive profile. Then it is totally up to her to find meaningful ways of doing so. For example, I will challenge her to go out into nature and pay attention to the animals, colors, landscapes, lakes, or whatever she likes to experience.

During the first week we discussed areas of the cognitive profile indirectly. Now I will challenge her to create a simple exercise that has limitless potential. The goal is to focus on a subject of their choice as long as possible while trying to understand it. It is important to engage her Self in the concentration as much as possible. This is always hard at first. Her thoughts will stray, and she will have to begin all over again. End results are not the goal when developing the cognitive profile. They do not matter. Repeating the exercise is what counts, especially for teens. The repetition strengthens their will! It is important for her to use her intrapersonal intelligence in a fun and valuable way. The goal is to focus her attention and create new experiences.

Where can she get started? A good start is to find something out of the ordinary that demands more willpower than usual. I challenge Carolin to concentrate on her horse's breathing when she rides. It sounds funny, but what counts in a simple exercise like this is that she make it work. She can focus on the rhythms of the horse's breathing as it moves. It is not as easy as it sounds, because she will continuously tune in and tune out. Learning to follow the flow and return to her goal of concentrating on the horse's breathing is extremely valuable, because she will observe herself in the process. She observes her power of concentration in a very enjoyable situation. Each time she loses her focus she observes that she is out of it. Then she refocuses on something that interests her. She learns! She challenges herself! After Carolin has practiced tuning into the horse's breathing when she rides, she can choose another exercise. For example, she can focus on a whole landscape. Once again focus is the goal. She certainly has a landscape she loves so that is a great place to develop her cognitive profile by unfolding her senses. As long as she finds the exercise meaningful, she will be willing to try and try again. You can read about this work in a landscape in her diary in Chapter 14.

Once she starts engaging her intelligences and her senses, there are limitless possibilities for her to enjoy. It is important for her to create her own methods. Of course, many kids do this without even thinking about it. The difference for Carolin is that she is doing it more consciously. She is integrating her experience of her Self by developing her cognitive profile in areas not accessible in the classroom. By working with her sensory perception, she balances the effects of her purely intellectual schoolwork.

New sensory perception is a valuable way for her to take her health seriously. By engaging her Self to experience nature, she gets to know it and can then use it to address the mental and physical sides to her problems. She needs to discover what pulls her down and what gives her strength. One way to do this is to be more selective in her experiences now that she does not have the pressure of school and her own exaggerated expectations of excellence. I challenge her to select which sensory experiences she wants to expose herself to. This helps her to engage her Self more fully in the experiences.

Another way to make teens aware of their Self is to challenge them to create an abundance of energy. They learn to differentiate between activities that make them weak and those that not only make them feel strong, but give them extra energy. This feeling is the result of their lifestyle, their way of thinking, their attitudes, and their actions. At the age of eighteen they can start observing not only their usual energy levels but also their abundance of energy. When Carolin creates a life style that gives her an abundance of energy, she overcomes the source of her body's exhaustion. She feels good about the fact that she can relax and take care of her body.

In New York it will be very important for her to continually create meaningful content—with this I mean productive thoughts and actions that she participates in. The city is a great place to do just that. The fact that she is actively engaged in the creation of meaningful ideas and actions strengthens her ability to engage her Self in a city that will otherwise overwhelm her.

How is Jason Doing at this Particular Moment?

Almost nothing Jason does this summer is determined by his inner disposition. For the most part he is just reacting to whatever comes his way. His work, his partying, his frustration about himself are all determined by outside expectations. Jason is steadily losing his way in the world. His parents' narrowness and his own weaknesses inhibit his personality development. The continual compromises with his parents create a lack of passion in his daily life. He fills his senses with violent and abusive junk on the screen. Part of his frustration is expressed in heavy drinking.

Jason's horizon is so narrow that he seldom speaks for himself. A long time ago, his father's constant criticism knocked most of the boy's courage out of him. As an unhappy misfit in his own family, he drowns in his love/hate relationship with his parents. He knows what to expect of his father every evening — the latest tirade!

Because both parents are ignoring the real issues concerning respect for their children's individual needs, all they have left is their ability to manipulate. Alex and Sharon are no longer trying to change themselves. They do not focus on the best in Jason. Nor are they aware of the consistent fear that grips his heart and dominates his thoughts. The boy seldom does what he really wants to do. Instead he has been conditioned to constantly compare himself to others and find himself lacking.

Jason dwells in emotional isolation. His anger is turned on himself. The lack of confidence and lack of content in his life combine with a number of bad attitudes to make his transition to young adulthood very complicated. I see multiple bad attitudes: cynicism, exaggerated self-criticism, and a willingness to let his parents decide his actions!

There is a clear maturity issue at work in Jason's case and, unfortunately, he does not see himself on the edge, even though he is. He hasn't met his Self. Because of the emotional abuse he has received at home, his self-confidence is not emerging. Rather than having the courage to push himself into a deeper understanding of himself and his friends, he has chosen to run from that process by drinking and indulging in useless entertainment that merely fill up his gaps. He becomes more and more superficial. If only the boy could wake up and see himself on the verge of self-destruction.

Many of Jason's friends are restless and insecure. On the surface these narcissistic youth may appear very much in love with themselves, but inside they are actually withdrawn from others and not at all in touch with themselves. A vast reservoir of hidden anger is slowly expressing itself in Jason's self-destructive attitudes and actions. At first, his friends hear bitter comments; later they see him acting irresponsibly. All of his friends are swearing like crazy, but in Jason's voice they occasionally hear an uncanny meanness. If this tone continues, our tormented teenager may live a life full of doubts and overwhelming loneliness.

These problems are not easy to identify when you first read his diary in Chapter 2. Picking up the real issues in a teen's story is extremely hard. Therefore, you may want to reread the chapter with his real issues in mind.

Jason lacks positive affirmation of the true potential of his personality. This summer his life is stuck in a routine of work, friends, and drinking. He is never satisfied. So in order to succeed, Jason puts on a pseudo-personality that appears always happy, always successful. But he continually meets the expectations of others rather than connecting with his own. Conformity is replacing the power of his Self and pushing him into becoming exactly like everyone else. He lives in an intense state of insecurity.

In the legend Narcissus looks at his own face reflected in the water. All Narcissus sees is his beauty, and he falls in love with his own face. The reflection deceives him, and he does not see his inner life, his pain, and his history. Jason is also deceived by his reflection—so much that he is well on his way to losing contact with his Self.

Unfortunately, Jason seldom acts on the advice he has received from his teachers, friends, and coaches. Nevertheless, let me show you how I would work with him. Which of the key factors would I approach short-term with him?

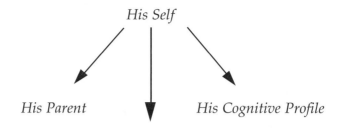

His Self

His Parent　　　　　*His Cognitive Profile*

His Cultural Background

As his mentor, I have to convince Jason that I have a new approach to adult contact so he will have more trust in me. If he wants to talk I will also hang out with him. I will have to be consistent in my contact with him. Then I can ask him a number of questions and bore down into some of the issues on his mind. My unspoken motive is to help him take his personality development seriously. I know that in his case every experience counts, and he has no time to waste!

Jason needs to break away from his parents, who are so immature themselves that they have resorted to parenting by manipulation. He does not need to break away from them finan cially or run away, but he certainly has to break away emotionally and morally. Jason has to take his own life in his hands and search for people who can help him create meaningful content. If I can help him trust himself more in the course of one week, then some changes will occur.

My goal is to help him move forward by developing new areas of his cognitive profile, but I will keep that to myself. I will tell him point blank that alcohol will only confuse him and that he needs to keep his head straight in order to get the most out of college this fall. The alcohol severely limits his contact with his cognitive profile. It makes him dull and weak rather than clear and strong. During the first week of our talks I challenge him to stop drinking and write down his thoughts instead.

A very productive way for teens to develop their cognitive profile is to write down their new thoughts. There are many invaluable elements in such a simple exercise. First of all Jason will create a dialogue with himself. In this way he engages more in his *sense of Self*. This exercise is not easy when alcohol is in the way, but he can break through this wall! The dialogue becomes stronger and stronger when he feels the haze lift and tries to figure out what is new in his thinking and what is old. Each day he has a flow of new thoughts in addition to a flow of old thoughts that merely pop up in the form of mental images. All of his mental images from the video games and from the movies flow freely into his mind. This week I want him to start sorting out those old thoughts so he can identify new ones in his mind. I want him to write down any new thought he has. Then the big step is to act on his new thoughts. His actions give him moral strength that reinforces the development of his cognitive profile. When he realizes that he is making progress through his own actions, he becomes stronger and then hopefully grasps other areas of intelligence and sensory creativity! His *sense of Self* unfolds!

Another area we can talk about during the first week is the narrowness of the popular culture he indulges in. I feel free to criticize counterproductive and destructive activities in his town. For example, I know that putting people down has been refined to an art form. Few adults have made an effort to get rid of their personal problems, and now their kids are being heavily exposed to it! Many adults, Jason's parents among them, lead a superficial life in their race for money. Their pursuit has left Jason to the video games and hours in front of the tube that he must now leave behind. They don't want him to think for himself.

Jason's cultural background is not supporting him. He has not tapped into the best of Pennsylvania, the best of America. Instead, he is a passive consumer with no drive for moving to the core of social issues, culture, or history. Therefore, his life lacks meaningful content and has become bad-tempered.

All of his passive activities need to be cut out and replaced by positive actions in which he sees himself creating his future.

No one else can do this for him. He has no excuses for being lost at the moment. The short-term challenges are as great as the risks at this crucial moment in his life.

Although I can achieve very few obvious results with the short-term strategy, I will work week in and week out to keep challenging him to create more continuity in his *Sense of Self*.

My **long-term strategy** entails key factors such as:

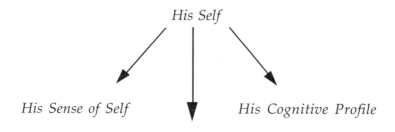

I will start with his strengths. It is a good sign that his father is upset about him searching for himself. There is no way back, and he should not live the life his father expects of him. He has a lot of goodness in him on which he needs to focus. He is smart and compassionate, and his sense of truth is strong. My goal is to teach him how to trust his own strengths and break into new experiences. To do so I must address the difference between his Self and his personality. If I am successful in making him aware of that part of his personality that gives him maturity and the confidence to change, I will have broken through the ice. Through conversations and exercises I will challenge him to search for the core of his personality.

When working with personality directly, I address issues related to attitudes. Jason needs to change some of his in order to create good experiences for himself! Changing attitudes is not easy because they lie deep inside and take time to address. I also have to discuss less positive aspects of his personality that I have observed, never an easy thing to do! After a couple of weeks I sense the trust between us is strong enough so that I can confront him about the bad attitudes that are pulling him down. I have to take this risk. It usually means hurting his feelings, and I risk losing meaningful contact with him.

The first step is to show him how he can work on his "who cares?" attitude. Behind that attitude is a mountain of fear, and I try to make sense of this! I give him clear feedback on what kind of messages he gives us with his drinking, swearing, and negative attitude about his sister. I play those messages back for him by repeating his words so he can see how he is coming across. Then I show him how he can change the attitude by deciding to focus on the positive sides of his life. To do this he needs to start developing new maturity. I will show him how to use his imagination to focus on what is important to him. He has a choice. Either he develops meaningful content in his life or he drowns in his lack of confidence.

How can he get in touch with his imagination? I challenge him to spend a week writing about where he wants to be five years from now. When we meet the next time, we can discuss his picture of the future and then go into many other opportunities he has. This exercise helps him open his horizon and gets him to talk about where he wants to go. He identifies obstacles in his personality.

Jason also needs to tap into his intrapersonal intelligence. His consciousness is not only polluted with violent media and too much alcohol, but it is also filled with abstract mental images that are not in tune with reality. If he continues on this path, he is at risk of not penetrating to the core of his personality to discover his true essence. Jason is isolated. Now it is essential for him to become involved in healthy group activities. He needs strong peers and concerned adults with whom he can interact and who in turn can bring him to the edge of his Self. In this situation you have to rely on your kid. You have to trust his unknown future.

A big step forward is needed for Jason to break out of his negative activities. He needs to let go of past experiences and move into new ones. This can only happen through the power of his Self. As a mentor my role is to support his initiatives in this area. I give him an exercise where he works with his memory. The goal is to observe past experiences as vividly as possible and then ask himself, "Was that experience valuable or not valuable?" This question avoids moralizing about himself and judging his actions as bad or good. No matter what the experience may be, he may find it valuable or not valuable. For example, we talk about the incident where he worked in the bank. I assume it created a certain amount of cynicism in him. Then I ask him to find the valuable part of the experience and the non-valuable parts of the experience. It helps to write down both categories of answers. Then he can let go of the experience by putting it in its proper place within his memory in his cognitive profile. Jason can do this exercise with many other experiences without hiring an analyst to interpret the issues for him. He does not need to focus on the heavy experiences or his traumatic issues with his parents. He deals with them later. I trust Jason. His Self is healthy but his *Sense of Self* is disturbed. It needs to be activated.

When growing beyond their starting points, teens build on first-hand experiences they have with all eight key factors of personality development. If they can learn from their experiences, they will go a long way. Carolin is good at this. She is striving to develop her cognitive profile and to learn from her health and family issues. For the time being Jason is floundering, but he can turn things around if he puts his mind to it.

Part II

The Teen-Adult Relationship

Introduction

Can adults improve their relationships with teens? Absolutely! That is what most teens are looking for. Whether we know it or not, they are already working on creating a new relationship with us. A few years ago, our teens saw through all of our strengths and weaknesses. With childlike grace they forgave us and carried on. They know exactly what we are thinking now and what we are going to say. One glance at our face, and they can see how we feel. They are much quicker than we are, and they know it. We will have a hard time fooling them. Our personality stands naked before them, and they are our mirrors, merciless mirrors. There is no escaping. Our only choice is to go further with our understanding of their lives.

What do we really mean when we talk about an adult co-operating with a teen? The teens you are living and working with are looking for the real you, behind all of the masks of your personality! Of course, your personality may be somewhat interesting and entertaining, but they want to connect with the power of your Self. If we cannot present our true Selves, teens move on.

The adult's Self is the mature mentor that can give the teen support and confirmation. With this support teens are in a better position to bring their own ideas and motives into their personality. When teens bring some of the strength of their Self into their actions, they can teach themselves to change attitudes, habits, mental images, or concepts. As adults we are challenged to focus on the teen's heart region that emerges in their inner lives between the ages of fourteen and eighteen. From the heart teens can truly speak for themselves.

In the following chapters, we will learn how to take off our blinders and discover the uniqueness of our teens. Adult blinders are fixed mental images about kids that appear in the form of expectations, dogmas, or frozen concepts from your past. These blinders prevent us from seeing our teen's personality development.

Part II of this book will help you focus on that which is new in your teen's life. You will learn how to pay attention to the "other heart" and listen better when teens speak for themselves. If teens ask you to be their mentor, you can guide them into their cross-currents and help them integrate their Self into the key factors of their personality.

All teens have life interests hidden within the core of their personalities. Only they can search for them, find them, and share them with others. All too often, the older generations prevent this from happening. It is not always in the establishment's vested interest to challenge teens to get in touch with their own ideals! Helping teens get in touch with themselves and their ideals is the essence of the teen-adult relationship.

CHAPTER 6

Breaking in the New Generations

The youth of today are not the youth of yesterday. As singer and songwriter Sara McLaughlin beautifully expresses , "Every generation yields a newborn hope unjaded by the years." As adults we have the pleasure of searching for that which is unjaded and unique in our teens. We can support their differences and challenge them to take the next step toward realizing their new-born hope. To do so we need to focus on the emerging Self in our teens and help them engage in that process.

Throughout history, apprentices have received help from their mentors or elders—wise and trusted advisors who took the time to listen, guide, or challenge their younger friends. These mentorships helped young people get in touch with their new-born hope. Adults passed on their cultural heritage and the tra-ditions that supported daily life. Masters of their trades taught teenagers practical skills, work ethic, and diligence. But teens were also taken advantage of.

Today, a productive mentorship can only be based on free initiatives taken by individuals in touch with their Self. The Self of the adult acknowledges the Self of the teen, and both give each other unbelievable strength! It may be built upon consis-tent, unconditional love between a teen and an adult. Some very mature teens can also give each other support that is just as valu-able. Together, they can work on common issues. They help each other make a new step in using their cognitive profiles.

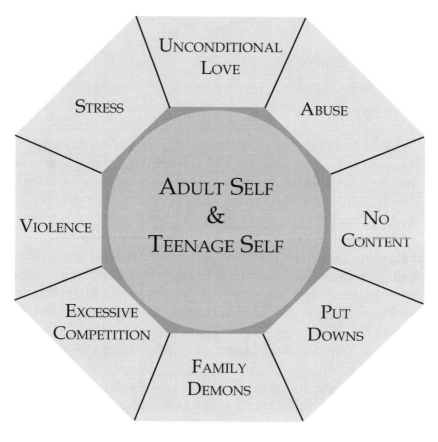

UNCONDITIONAL LOVE

STRESS

ABUSE

ADULT SELF
&
TEENAGE SELF

VIOLENCE

NO CONTENT

EXCESSIVE COMPETITION

PUT DOWNS

FAMILY DEMONS

Fig. 6

In this chapter we address seven general aspects of teenage emotional life through which adults can support change with *unconditional love*. If emotions are not worked on, they often reduce the teen's ability to unfold their intelligences and sensory experiences. The goal is to help teenagers break into society on their own terms. We create a supportive mentorship by helping them learn to manage *stress*, to release them from the conflicts created by the *family demons*, to overcome *abuse* in its many forms, and to help them find meaningful *content in their lives*. The goal is to teach positive reinforcement, so they can handle the *excessive competition*, the *constant put-downs* that life may present them at any time, and most of all transform the effects of first-hand and second-hand *violence*.

I envision this cooperation in the form of an octagon (see Fig. 6). With the power of unconditional love between an adult and a teen, the adult's Self and the teen's Self can mutually challenge, inspire, and support each other.

Stress

Let us look first at stress. Never before in the history of mankind have we had less work to do, more free time, more technology, more methods of travel, and more money at our disposal. Why then, is our lifestyle making people more and more stressed? We can write, call, fax, send e-mail, jump in a car, ride the bus, hop on a train, cruise on a plane, and sail on a boat, but still we feel isolated until we do something about it! Adults constantly complain about not having enough time or having too much to do, but teens are even more overbooked. High-achievers are obliged to do well in school, have good friends, be good at sports, date, play an instrument, and work part-time. The craziness is complete when you consider that most of the actions are geared towards future rewards!

Now we can do everything all at once—whether we are interested in it or not. Everyday we walk into our houses and decide which button to push! When we lose interest, we push another button. We spend hours reacting to stimulants rather than taking initiative ourselves. Our lifestyle lacks cohesion and productivity. Unfortunate habits take hold. One of the big ones is the habit of not really taking part in our actions. We end up doing things just for the sake of doing them, and we do not learn how to fully engage. Like adults our teens run around from meaningless action to meaningless action. When teens remain too long in this vacuum, they risk becoming totally disorientated in relation to time. They do not know what will happen next week, this weekend, or even tomorrow. And if I ask them to tell me something about last week, it is a big effort. That was ages ago, and they have forgotten most of it.

In all my years of teaching I never experienced a teen that did not benefit from a simple conference where I make sure to walk them through their relationship to time. Do you plan your homework? Do you plan your day? Do you know what is coming up next week and in two weeks time? It never stops amazing me how little consciousness teens have of time.

When I talk with them about stress, I usually take them through the dynamics of a stressful situation. We start with an exaggerated example: the teen has lost her wallet! It is a stupid mistake. And the panic makes it hard to work through the situation, step for step, in a logical manner. Temporarily, her concept of time is lost because she is stretched and pressed simultaneously. In order to find a better relationship to time, she has to think through her actions during the past hour. Where was she? What did she do? This exercise helps her concentrate on events in the stream of time. She also has to use her memory to see herself going through her actions in reverse. We talk through the actions she takes, so she can consciously observe herself in the situation. A lot of my pupils needed this guidance to wake up and carry out their daily actions with more clarity.

Many times I have asked parents and kids to go through their daily routines in order to help the early adolescent broaden her relationship to time. Mona merely needed to look at her daily activities and start to plan some of them in order to reduce her stress factor. At the age of thirteen her back was stiff and her temper short. We talked through her daily routines step by step from getting up in the morning until she came to school. Such details reveal an awful lot about teens. During the conference her mother also became more conscious of her patterns in time, attitudes, and habits that influence Mona heavily. The solution was simple, but it took time to discover it. It turned out that she delayed brushing her hair every morning and, therefore, had too little time to make the bus. This also made the first school lesson less valuable for her. What really mattered was the fact that her mother took her to the doctor to see how her back was doing, and they found a way to engage her in dance therapy three times a week. That really helped her relax.

For many teens stress is no problem at all. A certain amount of stress can be helpful. It can make them productive and push them into new achievements. I know teenagers who have too little stress in their lives and teenagers who have too much stress.

What I consider dangerous is "stress in stress." This occurs in teens when they not only are subjected to too much stress but major factors such as pressure at school, emotional problems at home, or personal setbacks with friends are added to their situation. Then the effect of stress increases exponentially. It lames and prohibits the teenager's personal development. If stress is allowed to develop into a major factor in a child's life, it may become a chronic problem with fear and depression as some of the results.

Many teens have emotional stress caused by "compelling-thoughts" that lock teenagers into a certain way of thinking. Such thoughts or mental images return day and night whether they are wanted or not. For example, they may be the result of peer pressure to experiment with drugs at junior high school, or they may come from unresolved problems at home. Because the recurring images appear instinctively, the stress factor is problematic. Popping uppers, drinking alcohol, or using prescription drugs may provide the escape from these uncomfortable images. Quite often teenagers who are stressed lash out at others and displace their anxiety on friends or family. Detachment may evolve from the "stress in stress" factor, and the teenager may escape into a self-made, fantasy world.

The schools also intentionally induce stress. Recently, I attended the parent evening at a local high school. The school principal kicked off the evening by saying that there were a lot of unhappy and stressed-out teenagers at the school and that the teens would have to learn to deal with this, because it is a part of life in the real world. "The sooner the better " was his attitude. Much too often stress is used by educators as a form of discipline, a power-game for them. They can control the kids by subjecting them to a stressful academic program. By repressing the students, teachers can make them behave! This pressure is also considered a good way of separating the good from the bad students.

Clearing out the Family Demons!

As an adult, you can make a major contribution to your teenager's future by cleaning out some of the *demons* you are carrying around. This is the garbage from your personal life that needs to be emptied! Whatever you want to call it, family demons prevent children from finding what they are really looking for in their lives. Those demons indirectly influence teens with bad attitudes and negative thinking. Teens will naturally assume the burden of their parents and the grandparents' triumphs and failures. The last things your teens need are your bad habits, your temper tantrums, and your unproductive attitude. What your personal garbage looks like, I cannot say. But you can figure it out and then decide what you want to do about it. If you discover one attitude you want to change and then actually do so, important progress will be made!

Whether we are conscious of it or not, our children and teenagers take on a lot of our ways of thinking, our manners, our values, our habits with good or bad, and sometimes even our fate. They take on all of this, as well as the scars that arise in their own generations. They love us and are more deeply connected to us than we realize. We are their mirrors, and as children they have imitated us and then learned from our authority, and now as teens they are defining their own lives. There is a limit to how much of the parents' mind-set and habits kids should take on!

Adults who have experienced the ravages of war easily pass down their trauma as bad habits or unsocial behavior to the coming generations. These family demons often take two generations to work out. The victims of war, the warriors, the photographers, and the correspondents all carry massively destructive experiences into their family life. I have seen many grandchildren and parents deal with bizarre behavior that the grandparents carry from their war experiences.

Should we decide to clear out some of our demons, we can begin by looking into our own years as teenagers. All of our experiences and feelings during our teenage years are somewhere below our daily consciousness, deeply asleep in the realms of memory. All we need to do is hear a song from those years and some of those feelings will arise. Then we will remember names and faces that populated our seventeen-year-old world. Our teenage years are like a brush fire that starts in one end of the field, smolders underground for a while, and surfaces unexpectedly. A little wind ignites the flames, and before we know it, we are smoking! If we continue to work in this direction over a greater period of time, we not only raise some of our experiences into consciousness, but resolve them, now out of the power of our Self at our present age.

I worked on my own personal garbage while my kids were small and discovered layers of cynicism from the late 1960s. I was very disillusioned with the abuse of man, the exploitation of nature, and the violence all around me as I grew up. I didn't like my attitudes, and I didn't want my kids to deal with my problems so I started studying American history from 1953 to

1981. I wanted to see what was happening at that time through the filter of my Self as a twenty-eight year old. I also went into my own lifetime year for year to see where I was when major events took place. I asked myself, "What happened in America when I was 14, 15, and 16? Who were the important people in my life during those years? While going backwards into my memory, I asked myself two questions: "Is this a valuable experience? Or is this experience not valuable?"

These questions gave me perspective on both good and bad experiences that I came across when trying to get rid of some of my garbage. I resolved many experiences, and I created inner freedom. My Self was able to work more powerfully into my personality, and my emotional life cleared up. I accessed more maturity and continuity in my actions. The gap between my thinking and my actions became consistently filled. I could better determine my actions, and I started connecting with my pupils. The teens I taught showed more interest in my methods of teaching and my approach to them.

Everyone has plenty of family demons to deal with. In doing so, we have the possibility of giving our teenagers a tremendous gift. We may even discover more compassion when we work through a small part of our life as a teenager and reach insights about not only the sunny parts but also the setbacks. Often it is a matter of learning to change our attitude. If we are able to release some of our demons, our teenager will notice it immediately. She will see that our attitudes are changing in small ways. For example, we react differently. We show interest in a new way. We see things that we did not see before. When our teenager has discovered that we have honestly changed, she will also grow from our change. The relationship between us breathes in a new way. There is fresh wind between us, and we can get closer or accept a distance more naturally. But this process has to be real. It may take years of hard work to create such a valuable gift.

Recently my own son became an officer in the Norwegian Army, which is the last thing I would have wanted him to do.

He has forced me to practice my own medicine. There is no lack of demons in my memory of the Vietnam War. We watched the war on TV every evening at dinnertime, so-called family entertainment. My father considered it part of our education. And we discussed the goals of the war with my father's friends. I was totally against it. They supported it. I developed an attitude that military training should be avoided. But now I have to honor my son's choice. I have never been where he is today! I am learning to respect his decision. And my respect will have to be real, or it will be worthless.

Our teenagers may even feel it their duty to carry out parts of our life that we did not fulfill. They may decide to take on a certain part of our fate, even if it does not belong to them. I have observed strong and idealistic teenagers who lost their parents at a young age go on to fulfill the career their parents were robbed of by sickness or death. A teen whose father died of a heart attack grows up to become a cardiologist. A woman whose mother gives up a career in magazine publishing grows up to become an accomplished editor. The unfulfilled potential of their parents ' lives is handed down as a challenge. Even in his absence, the father may have an enormous presence. While grappling with the death, the teenager struggles to make it whole, to make his father's life a part of his life. I know kids who decide that they want to pursue certain professions in order to fulfill that which was missing in their father's shortened life. This comes from loyalty and respect for the parents. But it can also lead kids down the wrong path in life.

The missing father is frozen in time. The teen unwillingly makes decisions to cover up fear. He still tries to please the father, to live him down and move beyond. Some of these teenagers discover themselves totally on the wrong track and then go through a dramatic change in order to find their own career, ideals, and life goals.

I have seen many teenagers who spend their lives trying to appease their parents. They have a great fear of rejection, of retribution, and of falling in the esteem of their parents. All too often, these fears become the motives for their actions, their choices in life. Appeasing others may become a habit that is carried over to peer-relationships. Jason is a good example. He just follows the crowd and does not try to discover his talents. In the end Jason risks spending his life worrying about pleasing everyone else, leaving him no chance to discover who he really is.

For teens it is not a question of having problems or not, but how they can learn to deal with their problems. Once teens have shaken off the garbage they have received from their parents, they can get to work on their own issues. Like fire on dry wood that has consumed its outer layer and then bursts forth, the individual begins to find his own path.

I often meet teens who are more mature than I was at their age. I find them fascinating. They have qualities I would have to spend a lifetime working on to make my own. They have more wisdom, more security, and more intelligence than I had at my disposal. I believe this maturity comes from the power of their Self. Looking at the best in them and seeing the vast potential makes me want to support their true strengths by removing more and more of my own demons.

Abuse

Another huge area in which we can support our teens as they move beyond their starting points is in teaching them how to deal with mental and physical abuse. The issue of abuse will cross every teen's path whether they have first-hand experiences or they live with those who carry the scars. There are many reasons for adults to take out their pain on their kids — none of which are legitimate. Three of the most common causes are drug and alcohol abuse, uncontrolled reactions, and family demons. The abuser either injures, dishonors, violates, or deceives a teen. Kids spend years of their lives in torment. Teach them never to accept any abuse, to confront it every time it occurs, and to speak to adults they trust whenever they are exposed to it.

Unfortunately, it is often extremely hard for kids to identify mental abuse and torment. Often the adults they love misuse substances and react to difficult situations with uncontrolled actions. Or family demons that have not been addressed by the adults return in physical or mental variations to punish the next generation. In this chapter I mention other subtle forms of taking undue advantage of teens: repeatedly undermining criticism, stress, unjust competition, and lack of content in the teen's life.

Lack of Content

Another major obstacle is not a poverty of the body, but a poverty of the soul. For many teens life seems to have no content. This condition may be observed all over town. It is just as present in the rich and middle class sections as in the poor sections. It is spread throughout the urban, suburban and rural areas. Its cause has nothing to do with money. A total *lack of content* in life is a state of affairs common to countless teenagers and adults all over the western world. When teens do not create a personal relationship to meaningful content in their lives, they drown in illusions and move from one meaningless activity to another. It becomes difficult to wake them up.

We share the responsibility for guiding young people into society. Each new generation of teenagers inherits the traditions and the policies of all of the institutions in their country. For better and for worse, they receive the results of the previous generation's actions. In addition to established institutions, teens are exposed to the unique heritage of their land, their people, and their language. This heritage inspires works of art, science, and religion. Walt Whitman described it with the following words:

"Subtly interwoven with the materiality and personality of a land, a race—Teutonic, Turk, Californian, or what-not—there is always something—I can hardly tell what it is—history but describes the results of it—it is the same as the untellable look of some human faces. Nature, too, in her stolid forms, is full of it — but to most it is there a secret. This something is rooted in the invisible roots, the profoundest meanings of that place, race or nationality; and to absorb and again effuse it, uttering words and products as from its midst, and carrying it, into highest regions, is the work, or a main part of the work, of any country's true author, poet, historian, lecturer, and perhaps even priest and philosopher. Here, and here only, are the foundations for our really valuable and permanent verse, drama, etc." [3]

Today, these foundations of unique creativity are not easy for teenagers to find. The invisible roots, the profoundest meaning of their land, their race, their nationality, need to be discovered and absorbed in an individual process before they can take it a step further. Where do we see this happening? During the teenage years we are often turned on to powerful authors and talented musicians. We may be inspired by our friends, teachers, or family to search for great people in our midst or in our history. We are introduced to powerful poetry and the ideas of an outstanding scientist. The skills of our craftsmen and the hard work of our tradesmen may also provide the inspiration to reach a more profound meaning. Whatever awakens our interest and passion may lead us down this path. But nothing is automatic. It is up to the individual whether or not this search is carried out over many years or forgotten. Cultural heritage is no longer passed down from generation to generation as it once was. In the past, the meaning of a people, of a land or of a language was experienced collectively. These days it is up to the individual to search for such meaning. An example is religion where we see the vast majority of teens searching for their own relationship to God.

We live in a time of tremendous upheaval in which individuals have become so strong that they are no longer dependent on groups and institutions. It is less important which class or side of town you come from, which profession and position you have, or how much you earn. Teens want to meet you. They want to know who you are and what you stand for, not what your name is, whom you work for, or where you come from.

The upside in this development is that teenagers, today, have to find out what they stand for. This inevitable change gives the individual the opportunity to create moral values based on freedom and integrity. The downside is that this is a very painful process, and the price being paid today is very high. But there is no way back now. Many teenagers live with the absence of the church, with missing parents, or with no moral education at all. Many are confused and inarticulate. And there is a greater difference between those who lead a productive life and those who merely drift through.

Today's teenagers are left on their own. They are forced to absorb extremely rapid cultural transitions. The vacuum can become a cultural wasteland or our teens can learn to create something new out of that nothingness. On the surface, history, religion, and the arts are out and money is in. The nihilism of entrepreneurialism has removed all obstacles, not only in the marketplace, but in our daily lives as well. These transitions in society are corrosive of all traditional and established truths. I call it "nothingness" because it creates a vacuum in each teenager's life. The vacuum will not be filled until individuals become strong enough to know what they want to create in their lives. They must then find the way to support each other in creating new social initiatives. We are being challenged to find the next step from the consumer society to new forms of human society in which truth is based on individual insight rather than the heritage of traditional groups. Once again, we are faced with a personal wasteland. Each day is nothing more than a meaningless response to outer stimulus. Each year brings the same behavior, the same entertainment, and the same passivity. Few people achieve any depth. The person has stopped thinking, stopped experiencing, and stopped striving. Such people may be well educated. I also meet them as professionals at high levels, but their lives are empty. If the individual does not ignite the fire of curiosity in the teenage years, then their poverty of the soul will be very hard to overcome later on in life. The friends you make as a teen can last a lifetime. So can the relationships you establish with music, literature, ideas, and many other activities undertaken as a teen. Those passions become sources of creativity teens can tap into throughout their lifetime.

What price are our teenagers paying during this time of upheaval? Adults are shocked when they hear about the reduction in learning levels and basic skills. Communicating clearly in written and oral speech is very difficult for half of our high school seniors. Math scores are substandard. Being able to think long enough to form and test a hypothesis independently is a big challenge for many teens today. And being able to read and write at the level of an eighteen-year- old may no longer be taken for granted. More than ever, teenagers have to work hard and consistently for many years in order to develop their ability to concentrate and express themselves. How many make the effort to do so? The magazines, television programs, movies, and other forms of popular culture seldom express something new and purposeful. They fill our time with distractions. The vacuum is then filled with unproductive activity.

The Constant Put-Down

Another major obstacle we adults put in their way is the exaggerated and well-refined way we *constantly put down* teenagers. Some of us are so negative that no matter what the teenager does, we tell them it isn't good enough! No matter how hard they try to please us, we are never satisfied. If parents continually put their kids down, the kids lose confidence and often choose to be good at being bad, rather then learning how to be good at being good.

When kids are constantly reminded that they are not good enough, there is always someone who is better! Kulia, a sixteen-year-old girl, was very aware of this. I talked with her one morning:

A friend of mine at school worked very hard on an assignment. She really gave her best. But when the teacher returned her work, he showed her how well another pupil had answered the questions. He said that she should try to answer just as well as the other pupil, and he said nothing positive about my friend's work. A lot us reacted to this treatment. We think it is a sign of weakness on the part of the teacher to compare her to the other pupil. Why is that so important? No matter what you do, it is not good enough. Our teachers compare us to others and point out how much better they are. We should be as good as them, no matter how well we have worked, and how hard we have tried. I think it is unfair.

This is a classical example of one generation teaching the next to criticize and put down each other. "You are never good enough" is the negative message used to break in the new generation.

One variation of the obstacle I have called *the constant put-down* is especially difficult for young people between the ages of eighteen and twenty-one, namely the constant comparison of the teen with everyone else in the world. It creeps up on many teenagers when they read the newspapers, the magazines, or watch television. It is the temptation to look at someone who is excellent in one area and compare him to yourself. They look around at all of the excellent achievements others have made, and they feel totally insignificant. No matter what they do, they experience themselves as useless and unimportant. This illusion is repeated time and time again in the teenage years. It comes from expectations and values set by the older generations. It is part of the game, but teenagers pay the price. Rather than feeling good about themselves and confident of their own destiny, they get lost in the comparisons with others. This demon creeps up when they are not expecting it, and they put themselves down. Very often the individual and the social standards are set unrealistically high.

These comparisons become exaggerated at the end of the teenage years. Just when the Self is struggling to become independent, many seventeen- and eighteen-year-olds experience themselves as unbeatable. They can conquer the whole world. Absolutely nothing fazes them. This sovereignty lasts a few short years until a new phase begins of freeing yourself from the past, your family, and society's superficial expectations. This new step in life is taken when the Self awakens at the end of the teenage years, usually near the age of twenty. This is a time when the child in you no longer protects the Self. Now the teen has to grow in direct relation to the experiences that are made in this lifetime, for better or for worse. The individual's mental and physical powers are coming into his or her own. They have strength of will that is unique during the whole life span. What is learned and dealt with in these years can be so strongly experienced and developed that the abilities may last for a lifetime. These are social, intellectual, and physical abilities that are acquired at this time.

But this is also a time of increased loneliness and independence. At this moment in our lives modern culture demands the standardization of individual attributes through dominance of SATs and athletics! Each teenager is forced to compete with every other teenager in the world. They compete intellectually to prove their productivity to future employers. They should instead search for knowledge that will give their life new depth. One unfortunate consequence of standardization is the process of securing their future according to society's values rather than their own. If teens trust their own values and ideals, they will be able to join the values of their society with individual maturity. To do this they need to learn to secure their unique, invaluable gift to mankind — their Self.

Excessive Competition

The need to compete excessively, to attain the highest standards of performance, to be supreme in their field of interest, is a constant challenge to adolescents between the ages of thirteen and twenty-one. In our society there is no way around this hurdle. It has to be jumped repeatedly during those years

The successful youth policies in sports, the arts, and academics concentrate on technical skills in the early teens. There are many factors that have to be coordinated to make a world-class achiever: massive talent and ambition, family support, an intelligent agent with a master plan, and the right timing. All of this is essential if you want to produce a millionaire. The competition is unrelenting. In many sports you are washed up by the age of fourteen if you haven't already made the grade.

The highest level of achievement is the basis upon which everyone is judged. There is nothing better than the best. In a competitive world the pursuit of excellence is the only way. But how realistic is this for the vast majority of young people? To be supreme in your field is a valuable ambition for some, but there are other qualities that count even more. The sheer joy of being involved in an experience cannot be characterized as good or bad. It carries its own inherent value. Great satisfaction may be experienced when you achieve your personal best. Teens can pursue new relationships, support their friends, create works of art, climb mountains, swim in the ocean, and walk on glaciers without any of it being judged by others. If they learn to feel good about their initiatives, they can inspire each other.

If they are constantly being put down at school, at home, on the athletic fields, and in the streets, they will become aggressive, angry, and do everything they can to destroy that which is tormenting them. And many end up destroying themselves.

In families and at schools we can work on competitive activities in which the teen not only competes against others but with himself upon his on premises.

By developing their cognitive profile and unfolding their senses teens grow as human beings, not as stars, successful students, or athletes. They do not need to be compared to others in these activities. They develop new skills if we give them the opportunities to do so.

Violence

The most devastating roadblock is set up whenever *violence* is spread from one generation to the next. In my experience nothing sits deeper in the teen psyche than the instances of first-hand violence witnessed in childhood and the teenage years. The imprint is so deep that the experiences continue to work year after year, decade after decade. The scars remain in the teen's emotional life, and they will depend on the power of their emerging Self to slowly overcome the influences as they grow older.

Knowing how destructive violence really is, it is surprising that we expose teens to so many experiences with it. Second-hand violence is one of the main sources of teenage entertainment today. The experiences in the media make deep impressions on the teen psyche but in a sneakier way. Violent sensations leave kids emotionally uninvolved. They get used to being apathetic when people on the screens are being killed, tortured, or misused.

Some kids "get pissed off" at school and go home to spend hours with violent videos. They take out their stress by watching someone go through even more of it. Some say this is a good way to channel aggression. Others consider it reinforcement of detached killing. Out-of-control behavior becomes acceptable.

Thousands of violent images and fantasies are taken into the teen's memory on a daily basis. Kids with violent tendencies entertain themselves with repeated hits of stress, abuse, and revenge. The terror they feel changes the flow of stress chemicals to the brain, and they shut down emotionally.

The destructive cycle of violence continues to turn even for kids who are not violent but expose themselves to too much second-hand violence in the media. Here it is extremely important to have a strong dialogue on the games they play or the movies they see. Moralizing will shut down your dialogue quickly, but asking questions in order to help your teen observe the sensory impressions he was exposed to by the media helps him tremendously. I like to ask my kids which movie they saw, why they liked or did not like it, what happened, what was the plot, etc. In this way I also help them work through their experiences. I even watch scenes on TV that I can't enjoy but that I can speak with them about later. The goal is to challenge them to judge their media experiences actively.

Unconditional Love

All of the emotional obstacles I have mentioned can be overcome when unconditional love flows between teens and adults. There is no more powerful tool for breaking in the new generations than unconditional love. This is the love that says to kids: "I love you for who you are. I care about you no matter how many mistakes you make. I don't care what you do in the future as long as you are happy. We are in it together." Carolin is fortunate enough to experience this with her mother. It is an essential source of self-esteem and confidence for her.

Conditional love is quite different. It says to kids: "Behave as I tell you and I will reward you. I love you as long as you meet my demands." Then adults create the conditions for receiving love. All kids can do is fulfill them! Freedom between parents and kids or teachers and pupils is not respected when love is conditional.

Unconditional love is essential not only in the home but in the community. From it evolves a sense of trust, common values, and the willingness to intervene in the lives of kids outside your family circle. Unconditional love between adults and teens is the foundation upon which our future will be created. It is the core of the teen-adult relationship. Without it teens will be severely limited as they work with the key factors in their personality development. In the following chapter we will see how teens experience the emergence of their Self. In order to follow your teen as she goes through this process, you will need to focus on that which is new in your teen's life.

With the power of your love and respect for your teen, you can work through parts of your personality that prevent you from perceiving. I call these areas that prevent your perception and your insight "blinders."

Chapter 7

Take Off the Blinders

Every day teens present themselves in unexpected packages. These may make us uncomfortable, but the changes are most excruciating for them. Jason is a good example. He makes his parents very uncomfortable because he is not fitting into their way of life. Nor is he strong enough to break out on his own. When he attends Penn State, we can only hope that he will awaken to the real strength in his Self that is temporarily hidden by his cynicism and defeatist attitude.

How often do we really know whether the teenager is bringing out the best in himself? Not very often. Why? Our fixed mental images, what I call blinders, usually prevent us from seeing the real situation our teens face. Mental images arise automatically in our minds. They come from our past. Our mental images are conclusions we made previously, and they often reflect how we want our teenagers to act. We want them to make the right choices about school, relationships, drugs, and alcohol. We want them to concentrate and read books. That is all very fine, but these decisions are not up to us. During the teenage years each kid needs to define his own relationships. We can't force kids to succeed.

Our own mental images of our teen's development provide guidance only if we continuously search for new images of their true situation. This is more difficult than it seems. As a teacher or parent we are daily challenged to keep up with them! In this chapter I will describe the basic steps in taking off our blinders so we can see our kids more clearly and support them more realistically.

The first thing to remember is that we can have any mental image we want, but the teen's perspective is more valid than ours. Asking questions about their perspective keeps us much closer to their reality than our limited mental images.

In my experience the parents are usually the problem, not the kids. Their parental blinders often mislead them. We think we know what is going on in our teen's life. More curiosity and uncertainty would help us get closer to their reality. Our uncertainty forces us to search for the teen's point of view. Only then do we feel the emotional force with which they believe in their views. If we honor the differences between us, we can better see how they think and view the world.

If anybody can help you take off your blinders, it is your teens. If anybody can identify your limited mental images, it is your teen. They know what you are missing out on, and they know each and every stupid habit, every wrong thought or bad attitude you have. All too often, adults try to save face by ignoring the signals they receive from children and teens. While adults have years of experience to work with, kids have untouched sources of spontaneity. But very often adults see only what they want to see based on past experiences rather than on what the teen is experiencing this moment. If parents do not work through some of their mental images, they will also lose spontaneity.

As a teacher I noticed that my pupils got over problems we had in the classroom quicker than I did. By the next day the issue — whatever it was — was in the past for them. I still struggled with the same issue. As a forty-year-old I have twenty-seven more years of mental images in my memory to let go of than a thirteen-year-old does. This batch of experiences is a major problem for adults who want to connect with kids on their level.

Fernanda, a high school senior in Boulder, Colorado, speaks about a lack of understanding:

"Nowadays kids are more intuitive and independent than their parents were. Kids actually learn faster, mature faster, and change faster than adults. Parents seldom see the changes and then the kids suffer from lack of understanding. As a teenager you are trying to find a balance. You have to experience the extremes on both ends in order to know where you stand. Teenagers do not hit a balancing point and stay there. They are constantly spinning."

Fernanda points to the spontaneity and experimentation among teenagers that is beyond the comprehension of many adults. If we are not interested in discovering something new about our teens, we will not put ourselves in a position to meet them in their process of change. Very often it is our attitude that keeps us from making the effort. If we do not take off our blinders, our teens will either rebel against us or resign themselves to the fact that we are not capable of change. Without significant changes in our relationships with teenagers, they may be forced to turn their back on us. The question may arise: Who is being unfair to whom?

Blinder #1 The Individual is Not Respected

If a school wants to remain the same school, year after year and decade after decade, that is its choice. If the family wants to remain the same old family, from generation to generation, that is also a possibility. But not always will individuals in that family fit in. How often do we hear variations of the following statement Oya once expressed?

"My family will never accept my opinion because their culture, their traditions, their thoughts always have to be the right ones. I can not find common ground with them, and there is no room for compromise."

In traditionally authoritative cultures, teenagers are punished for rebelling. They are forced to shut up, ridiculed for their differences, sometimes abused, and all too often sent out on the street when they do not comply.

On the other hand, lenient parents have a tendency to accept all kinds of behavior and not set any boundaries for their teenagers. Their blinders are often colored by lack of judgment or a shortage of real concern. This inability to set limits also shows a lack of respect for the individual. I worked with one boy from an extremely relaxed household. He could decide, for example, whether or not he wanted to come home at night, whether or not he would go to school. I felt sorry for Truls, but I also had to be tough with him in order to help him wake up. By the age of fourteen Truls was losing his faculty with language. He was pale and unhappy. Why? Because he had to take on all of the decisions his parents should have been making. He was turning old because of the so-called freedom he had. Truls was mean to his little sister, and he eventually exploded at his mother one night by hitting her! A couple of weeks later he told me he was listening to some heavy music when the brutal message from the music got through to him. He said he fell on the floor rolling in pain from the aggression in the music. When he got to his feet again, he realized he wanted to cut out that kind of music and lead a different kind of life.

Blinder #2 The Pressure Game gives Rewards

Do as I say and you will be rewarded. Act as I expect you to act and I will be your friend. These attitudes are counterproductive in the teenage years. Nor do they work for small children. Conditional love puts pressure on kids to comply. It is a form of manipulation. This game has many faces. Judy, another observant senior in Boulder, described the pressure game for me:

> Parents put more pressure on their teenagers at an earlier age than in the past. That is because the parents do not see the real-world problems teenagers are facing today. Ninety-percent of all families do not eat meals together anymore. Parents pay the bills, and all the kids do is react. The reason parents put such pressure on

their teenagers is because of the influences from their own parents. The grandparents play a major role in the pressure game. Look at how the parents were raised. Our problem is often the fact that adolescents end up raising adolescents. My parents' parents did not let them do what they wanted to do. Now my parents try to pressure me into going to college in order for me to be able to do what I want to do. A college degree does not go as far as it did in their days. First, I want to go to Africa after high school and learn to be a midwife. Quite often parents do not see you as the person you are. They think you are a good person because you are good in something. Kids show that the parents have done a good job. But the children have no say in the matter. Their feelings play no role at all. There is no balanced point of guidance.

Teens who are under this kind of pressure from their parents may have a very complicated life. For example, I have seen parents like Alex and Sharon who not only live through their children but, at the same time, are jealous of them. Parents want their children to meet their demands because they consider their kids a threat. For example, the teen may be more intelligent, more social, or enjoy life much more than the parents and, therefore, the parents create a very complicated form of pressure that is geared at keeping the teenager in place. Loyalty conflicts arise for the teen. Manipulation, instead of cooperation, flourishes.

Jason is struggling with a loyalty conflict. Alex and Sharon have put Jason in a pressure cooker designed to make him fulfill their dreams while preventing him from becoming any better or more successful than themselves. They want him to lead the life they lead and, therefore, do not try to challenge him to do something new. They don't look for the original aspects of their son's personality. Nor do they know how to deal with his passive behavior. He is a threat to Alex because he does not want to follow in his father's footsteps. So Alex repeatedly pressures him psychologically. This is not a conscious effort by the parents, but the manipulation is effective. We see this in his lack of confidence and the way he lets his father push him around on the tennis court and at home after the match.

Blinder #3 We are Totally Out of It

When I try to work with adults like Alex, Sharon, Tommy and Karen, the first thing I tell them is that they can discover new sides of their lives. I tell them that they are wearing blinders that are creating blind spots in their dealings with their kids. I let them know that they are clueless as to what is really going on in their kid's life. My goal is to go into detail with them but just how far they let me is often very limited.

Take Tommy as an example. His blind spots are in his attitudes and habits he uses to make it through the day. Work is the most important part of his life. It is poisonous for his kids to know that he does not really appreciate them. He is so distant that they know he doesn't really care any more. This acts like a poison in their emotional self-esteem. They can't even count on him keeping his promises. If I can convince him of the fact that he can move in new directions, I have accomplished a lot. My goal with Tommy is to get him to accept the following three steps in changing his destructive behavior.

Step 1   Admit he has blinders
Step 2   Be willing to take them off
Step 3   Toss out his old ways of relating to his teen

Once he moves through all three steps, he can turn in a new direction. If he trusts me, I can lead him through these phases. A number of the parents in my classes have been successful over time. My advice for Tommy is to get close to Carolin no matter how painful it may be for him to discover his guilty conscience. She will probably not trust him at first, so he will have to prove his worth to her. As I mentioned before, she is usually a step ahead of him when they speak. This is fun for her. She also likes to make comments that throw him off balance. Remember how she spoke with him on the first morning at the shore. She hid everything from him and brushed him off with a few comments. Carolin doesn't really respect him anymore, so she is not afraid of being unfair to him. She sees that he is stuck, and she knows she is powerful, so she tries out her emotional strength on him by talking about things that are uncomfortable for him—his job, his mother, his love life—whatever comes up. As a parent he should feel honored to have her play out these tactics with him because it gives him the chance to teach her what is fair and what is unfair. He can use the opportunity to help her learn how to speak for herself. The problem is that he seldom speaks for himself. I can tell that is something he has never taken seriously.

Unfortunately, he chose to ignore Carolin in her early teens so that she had an even tougher time at school and at home. She has taken on a lot of the responsibility for her sister and her mother while he ignored the family. She filled the adult role in her early teens instead of exploring life like her girlfriends. Carolin became serious and burdened by insecurity in her family life. She reacted by becoming an over-achiever at school, always in need of pleasing the teacher and getting the best grades. The symptoms of stress and fatigue are clearly seen in her regular loss of energy. Many first children in dysfunctional families take on so much responsibility at an early age that they lose part of their youth. Patterns are set, and they often lack flexibility and endurance. Still, it is not too late for him to reach her. But he has to move quickly!

The same is true of both of Jason's parents. They have a lot to learn. There is a lot of denial and fear to overcome if they are to deal with him honestly.

It is extremely important to interact with your teens out of the power of your Self. Kids need the mature Self of an adult to grow with. That is what they are really looking for in you—not just your money, your personality and your friendship. Your

Self is the source of true adult supervision in the teenage years. If you meet your teens out of the power of your Self, they may cooperate in new spontaneous ways. Be they aloof, be they arrogant, be they a raucous, undisciplined bunch, you can continue to interact with them effectively when you know what you are looking for and you are in touch with the power of your adult Self. This is the only way you can give them a healthy sense of security.

Three boys I worked with over four years come to mind when I think of the need for a mature adult Self. Jake and Paul have no fathers, and Bill has serious personal problems despite great parents. We spent almost every day together at school for eight years. We focused on moving forward and cooperated on good habits, good attitudes, and productive social actions. I noticed they were right there, no matter how I felt or struggled. They supported me, and I supported them. The daily turmoil was hard on the whole class. I noticed that kids who go through a long struggle together with an adult give the most unbelievable gift—their trust and respect. They share their fate with the adult who carries them through. They give great strength and love. And the rest of the class notices it. It inspires everyone.

If I take the time to be perfectly honest with myself, I admit that, in relation to the teenagers I work with, I have a number of blinders I put on every day. For example, I easily get caught in my memory of the emotional effects of their previous actions. This makes it difficult to see new actions they display. Another example appears when outer appearance deceives me. At times I am fooled by how they act and things they say. My biggest blinder concerns violence. When I see kids hitting each other or groups yelling at each other, I quickly become emotionally involved and lose a certain distance to the situation that will help me deal fairly.

Therefore, the best starting point I have found is to admit that I am out of it—totally out of it! This point of view can at least set my reflections in the right direction. It softens the edge of my ego and opens unknown territory because it is an excellent starting point for a learning process. I ask myself repeatedly, "Now, where do I go from here?"

Blinder # 4 The Whole Truth and Nothing but the Truth

Many people are convinced that whatever they experience and see in the course of a day is the whole reality. They do not search for more. Everything presented at home, on the street, at school or work is the reality they accept as final. It is the whole truth and nothing but the truth. All they choose to do is to continue to relate to the given reality. Period. Alex is one of these guys. He has narrowed his reality to include his way of life, his convictions, and his habits. He couldn't care less how that affects Jason. What he is looking for is a son who will do what he does, only do it better.

As far as teenagers are concerned, this concept of reality entails a serious limitation to their existence and their future. A major part of their life will not be taken seriously by anyone who is convinced that reality is only what you experience with your senses. I experience this conviction as the most popular blinder that exists today. Tommy has it. He is coasting into the future even though his kids want to cruise! It is very comfortable for him to lead a narrow life. He has no interest in questioning his attitudes, changing his habits, and learning to think in a new way. The fact that he is alienating his kids does not bother him. Tough luck for the kid's attitude.

It would be a major accomplishment to get Alex, Sharon, and Tommy to work with the eight key factors of personality development. That is not going to happen. Only a crisis could get them to open up to the true potential of their cognitive profiles, for example. They have chosen to limit their horizons to the experiences they meet every day. That has become their whole truth.

Blinder #5 What are your Preconceptions?

A very simple way for Tommy to improve his relationship with Carolin is practice asking himself questions when they are together. This will improve his ability to observe Carolin.

Let us say that Carolin appears on the porch one afternoon on the shore. The goal is for Tommy not only to notice his preconceptions arising in his consciousness, but the flow of his opinions, prejudgments, and mental images. These are his blinders, and they are not easy to discover. Some people think this is impossible, but it is not! Tommy can actively observe Carolin in the moment, without prejudice. To do so, Tommy can allow the initial, habitual images to appear but then make a big effort to try to see more. What does he really see? There is much more than meets the eye. Carolin is much more than her father can see with his immediate senses. In this moment, Tommy can go a step further by asking himself a question. "What is she really thinking?" This simple question challenges him to show interest in what may be new in her life. New in this moment! She may have new insight, new feelings or new problems to express, though none of this has to be verbal. He searches for new, meaningful relationships in his observations. It takes a big effort, but it is fun, too! Teens who notice me doing this greatly appreciate my efforts.

If Tommy repeats this little extra exercise, he can get good at it! He can ask more questions:

What do I see in Carolin right now?
What did I see during the course of the week?
What do I really know about her thoughts these days?

The awareness helps Tommy bring the power of his Self actively in the process. He connects with Carolin. And you can be sure that she will notice the changes in him.

Such a simple experiment can help us review the unconscious judgments that habitually accompany our way of looking at the world. In this way, we can learn to add information and thereby overcome some of our biases. Many of our opinions are based on prejudices we have. Prejudices are dependent upon the position from which they are taken. The more we think about our opinions, the weaker the influence of our biases and prejudices become. We free ourselves to find new angles from which to view the teenagers with whom we are living and working.

Many people have discovered this process after going through hard times and illnesses. They are often forced to see life and those they are living with in a new way. Actually, it is a way of showing respect for another human being with whom we are living and working. When we practice taking off our blinders, we can see the three big steps our teens take, as outlined in the following chapter.

CHAPTER 8

Three Big Steps

If I am lucky, I usually tune into my teens a few weeks after they have changed. Without noticing it I suddenly have to deal with a whole new person. My son shows me he is an independent thirteen-year-old by putting me in my place! Or my sixteen-year-old daughter is exploring new avenues of her personality! She talks differently. She walks differently. She is interested in new people! At school I have also taken off my blinders and discovered eighteen-year-old pupils that are suddenly mature, full of insight, with good priorities and continuity in their thinking.

Those who observe carefully discover three phases of teenage personality development: early, middle and late adolescence. The first phase of development is their awakening to their intellectual resources around the age of thirteen. The second is the awakening to the evolving personality around the age of sixteen, and the third regards the emergence of the Self around the age of eighteen.

Abstract Thinking — Early Adolescence

Let us first look into the new phase of teen's thinking that appears roughly at the age of thirteen. Adults may observe this change as the teen's new ability to grasp words and indulge in logical arguments. You can also see the significant change clothed in common tactics teens use to turn their arguments against adults. Once you start arguing with an early adolescent, you are in for trouble. Sometimes it is great fun, and other times it becomes a battle because they are in it to win!

Early adolescents are also ready to develop their logical, systematic thinking. They start to understand the world with abstract concepts. My fourteen-year-old son asked me recently while driving in the car if they had ever dropped the bomb. I said, "Yes, twice." He replied, " How many did they kill?" Childhood innocence disappears in a radical way when they awaken to their critical thinking. You can notice it in the questions they ask.

In early adolescence teens become more differentiated in their reflections as well as their actions. They become self-critical because their thinking is more abstract, and they are able to see themselves from the outside. That is not always a comfortable experience for them.

Jason wrote the following lines in his diary at the age of fourteen. I suggest you notice how he reflects upon the situations he experiences. He is becoming critical, which means he is leaving his childhood behind and entering into the teenage struggle for self-esteem. In the process he is turning into a positive kid with a lot of resources.

> In the bottom of the ninth inning, with men on second and third, I slashed a high, outside fastball down the first base line into deep right field. By the time I rounded second base, the game was over. I trotted back to the bench filled with excitement. Just as I shook hands with the coach, my teammates jumped all over me. We won the game!
>
> Later that evening, as my Uncle Joe put a huge T-bone steak on the grill, he told me he was proud of me out there. He and my Aunt Tina came up from Philadel-

phia for the summer, while my parents are gone on their annual one-month summer vacation in the Adirondacks. Uncle Joe and Aunt Tina are a second set of parents. They like to play around a lot.

That summer all I wanted to do was stay in Pennsylvania and play baseball. I love the game! My throwing arm is not great, but I can hit the ball. Whenever I come up to the plate, my teammates know I will get on base. In the field, I love catching fly balls on the run, especially when I rob the batter of a great hit!

In between games I paint houses. Like most other kids in the Poconos, I swim all summer long. These hills are paradise.

After dinner that evening, I watch some TV and munch Snyder's pretzels. Then I go to bed early. As I lay in the humid room, listening to the familiar crickets and the laughter from the terrace, I think about the game. That evening I fall asleep smiling about the hit into right field. I just close my eyes and repeat the feeling again and again—with full power.

Friday afternoon we pick up my best friend Mark and drive down to the Martz terminal to get on the bus for Yankee Stadium. I haven't been there since last year, and this is exciting because the Red Sox are in town, and they are hot. But so are the Yankees and Petitte has the start tonight!

We sit behind the driver, who tells us all about his variable-vane-torque convertible with two turbo chargers that make the bus move swiftly up East Mountain in third gear. Everything is fine as long as the computer works, he says. Across the isle a grown-up lady is playing her child's game-boy. The idiotic sounds irritate the hell out of me. And the smell of the bus reminds me of a leaking soap-bottle on wheels!

They turn on the movie—something uneventful. In my mind, though, I am already outside the stadium feeling the rush of looking through the gate onto the luscious green field and taking in the sounds of the thousands of fans in their seats getting ready for the opening pitch. But we are two hours away, and the bus finally shifts into fifth gear and picks up some speed into the Poconos. Lake Scranton is left behind us, and we are starting to roll. The driver shifts into sixth gear!

Mark has a hundred questions as usual. I like that. He knows more statistics and facts about the game than I do. Mark is a long-time Yankee fan. His curiosity also takes off into the social scene. Who is working where? Who is dating whom? And he usually has some juicy numbers about the older generation's scandals! You think we are crazy. My parent's generation is really out of control. We have some serious nut cases in town. Just go to a cocktail party and make the rounds shaking hands with the stars of the show. Talk about hitting the bottle! You know. They have a cig in one hand and a tall glass of whatever in the other, and it takes time to put the cig into the hand holding the glass without spilling the juice. Once they carry out this balancing act, the right hand is free because the cig and the drink are finally in the same hand. You get good at that after some of these parties. Of course, they love to see you again, but they don't have much to say, and they aren't really interested, except one or two that look you in the eyes and show genuine curiosity.

I'm not really into the movie, so I start looking for cops hiding beside the highway, and I make sure to keep the gossip with Mark rolling. He is a great storyteller, and he likes to laugh. We get a little out of control, and the girls behind us ask us to hang it outside so they can follow the movie.

After driving through New Jersey for almost an hour, we cross the George Washington Bridge and head into the Bronx. The driver starts taking some fancy turns, and before we know it, he swings the bus into a high-fenced parking lot three hundred yards from Yankee Stadium. It turns out the bus driver is from the Bronx. That is why he knows so many short cuts. He told me he moved to the Poconos to get out of the city. I can understand that!

We enter the ballpark and find our seats on the third base line. The excitement is in the air — Yankee Stadium — the center of the world! I love it when the subway flies by the right field bleachers! Somehow that makes me feel at home. Andy Petitte is warming up in the bullpen in left centerfield. The other guys take batting practice as I walk around the stadium to get some other views. I hope they never tear this baby down. Think of the history that has taken place here!

The Yankees play a great game. Bernie Williams drives in the winning run with a two-out single in the bottom of the ninth. We leave the stadium in the dark and find the bus.

After a couple of minutes driving through the Bronx, the driver sweeps full speed up a steep hill and makes a swing at high speed to the right. This time though, there is a group of guys on the sidewalk playing cards on a fold-up table. He drives right at them full speed into the swing, and the jaws of the card players drop! They have a bus coming right at them! The guys panic and run away as fast as they can. Our driver misses the table by some inches. We all scream! It is right out of Hollywood. All the driver can say is "That was close! Good thing we didn't stop!

Two weeks later my parents came home from their vacation. Unfortunately, late that same afternoon my father and I play tennis with some friends. Second best is never good enough for him. After a long career in tournaments, he still finds pleasure in winning on the tennis court. My game can be summed up in two phrases — a powerful groundstroke and an erratic serve. We start out slowly and lose the first set 6-4. Dad asks for a longer break so he can light up between sets. I don't think that will help us much. Half way through the second set he starts taking chances and lucks out with some great shots down the back line. He signals to me, in his usual way, to serve harder. So I hit my second serve as hard as my first. It works three times before I back off. That gave us the second set. In the break before the final set, he lights up again while I dry off my hands and racket to improve my grip. As we walk onto the court again, I notice his eyes are glaring and his lip is curled in a very ugly manner. He turns to me and growls, "I really want this next set so you better not blow it!" I smell his sweat as I try to get out of the way. I blurt out, "Get on your own case — not mine!"

We start out winning the first two games, and things look good. Then Alex loses his serve and starts getting mad at himself — swearing and stomping around. In his relentless way, he ridicules me with stupid comments each time I walk up to the net. I guess it is well intended. He says he only wants my best. But I am relieved when we win the next set and head for home. A couple of years ago I had more fun playing with him.

In Jason's diary we see many good attitudes. He is outgoing and adventurous. The boy goes into details whether it may concern the transmission on the bus or the driver moving to Pennsylvania. He loves Yankee stadium — a place where he can experience appreciation for great athletes and games.

At home he is critical of the superficiality of the cocktail circuit. He is aware of his distance to his parents. And most importantly, he enjoys life!

Dealing with peer approval takes on new importance for early adolescent teens. The new distance between the child and his environment brings both doubt and independence. The distance is a foundation upon which the free individual will build throughout the teenage years and early adulthood.

Many suffer from insecurity about their appearance. Increased self-consciousness and egocentricity often make early-adolescents think that everyone is looking at them. They often feel like outsiders. If exaggerated self-consciousness continues, they will have many solitary years in which they show no emotion. I have noticed many teens become less assertive at this phase of adolescence. Their grades may drop, while they are more inclined to take risks in other directions.

At this age, teenagers often operate out of resistance. They know what they want to say, and they have good reasons for their comments. Their ability to grasp new facts and then learn to see the relationships between the facts is being developed. At school they start the long process of being confident that they are good in each subject. Teachers need to bring the learning process to the point where the teen is confident in her knowledge of the subject. Knowing that you know a subject or even a small part of a subject is supportive of the entire personality development and the emergence of the Self. It is one of the essential building blocks to self-esteem, confidence, and security. If the teen is unsure of what she knows, problems set in. Each time she is unsure of what she knows, confidence and security are temporarily set back.

Early adolescents love to create opposition, and they are often entertained by our reactions. It is a game they play with us. Not every argument is fair, not every comment well founded, but once again the way to learn is by trial and error. It takes years of practice before they learn to speak for themselves more consistently from their own heart.

We can observe this ability in a very special moment that every parent will remember. It is the first time your teenager criticized you with such power that you had no response! This power comes from the awakened intellectual capacity for thought that usually occurs around the ages of thirteen or fourteen. For example, when Carolin has the strength to say, "You may be in a bad mood today, but not at my expense!" her parents may react: "Who is this new person in our family?"

Quite often early adolescents need to learn what messages they are giving others. If I want to help them improve their communication skills, I usually ask them some fundamental questions:

What message are you giving here?

What role are you putting your parents in?

What role are you putting yourself in?

When they answer such questions, they learn that it pays to be honest.

In early adolescence teens become personally responsible for their actions. Not only will they meet the people they need to meet, but they will also begin the process of creating their own future. Every encounter counts. Every phase is critical. The teenage years fly by! Can we find a picture that represents the flow of change from early adolescence to the middle and late phases?

The picture I prefer for teenage personality development is the water lily! It has its roots underneath the murky waters under the floor of the lake. Its flower breaks the surface of the water, then it opens and closes itself according to light. The opening and closing in response to light reflects the emergence of the Self during adolescence.

Early Adolescence
(Ages 13 - 14)

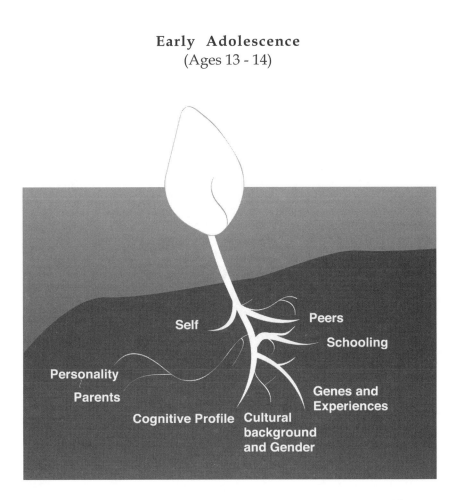

Fig. 7

In this picture we find all eight key factors of personality development represented as the roots of the lily. As the Self emerges and the personality unfolds, the key factors change in their relation to each other. These changes will become clear when we bring the picture into the middle adolescent period (ages 15 –17) and then the late adolescent period (ages 18–21).

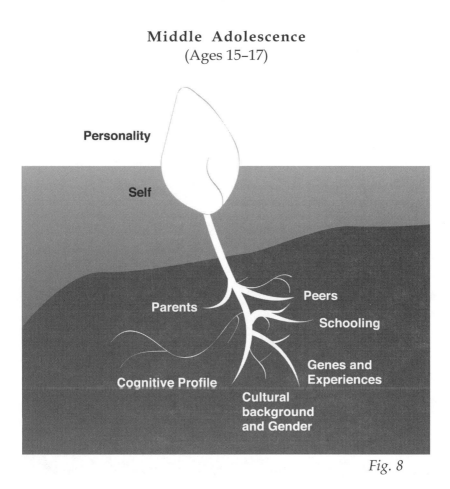

Fig. 8

This picture shows changes in the eight key factors of personality development. The personality has surfaced. It is in full bloom compared with the other key factors that continue to provide the roots for further development. The Self has not yet fully emerged. It is still below the surface but it emerges into the personality where it continually unfolds. It will do so throughout the late adolescent phase.

Middle Adolescence

How can we observe the personality as it surfaces? We need to look for changes. This excerpt from Carolin's diary will give you the opportunity to identify her new ability to reflect at the age of sixteen.

I knew something was happening! That bright April morning two years ago is clear in my memory. I walk briskly into the kitchen, turn on the radio, and tell Erin, my little sister, to eat her breakfast quickly so we can walk to the school bus together. In fifteen minutes we have to be at the bus stop. Without pausing, I pull the carton out of the refrigerator and pour myself a tempting glass of Florida orange juice. Nothing like it! Then I mix a bowl of Cheerios with a banana and some yogurt before carrying it over to the breakfast table. I pull up a chair, sit down, dump some milk on the Cheerios, and turn on the radio. We didn't want to speak that morning. Erin was about done, and she was a little irritated with me.

"What is the rush?" Erin questions. "We have plenty of time. Relax. We have two busses we can take. I just read the sports page and they have a nice article about my two-hitter with 10 strikeouts against Riverside. Want to see it?"

I look up! "You're kidding. Let me see it." Balancing the newspaper awkwardly in my left hand, I scoop up the cereal with my right. It is a pleasant surprise to read about my sister's triumph in the sports pages of the *Scranton Tribune*.

Erin leaves the table and disappears upstairs to get ready. I skim the rest of the paper, finish my juice, and scrape the bottom of my bowl like a good girl. No time to waste. I jam the dishes into the washer and stomp off towards the stairs.

Rounding the corner at the bottom of the stairs, I remember that I didn't sleep very well last night. Actually, I feel like a ton of bricks running up the stairs. Suddenly, my dream from last night flashes into my memory! In a split second, as I pass the final step to the second floor on my way to the bathroom with five minutes left before I will leave the house, the flash in my memory from my dream brings me back to an incident four years ago, when I found my mother laying stunned in her bed. She and my dad had just had a fight. My reaction then was to tell her to do what was best for her. As I walk down the hall and open the bathroom door, the vivid pictures of the usual drag out fight between my parents chills my mind. Another one of Tommy's profanity-laced tirades had hit her. I remember it like yesterday. This garbage! I'm so fed up with their problems.

I take out my toothbrush and try to clear my head of the ugly memory. The familiar taste of Crest toothpaste brings me back to reality. After spitting out the toothpaste, I grab my hairbrush and check the time on my watch. If I push it, I can brush my scattered, dark brown hair. As I bend back my head with every long stroke, I decide to ignore myself and get on with the day. But I could not escape glancing at my face in the mirror. Ohhh! My eyes show signs of fatigue. That is definitely not what I like to see, so I pivot quickly and head down the stairs.

My schoolbag lies by the door, untouched since yesterday. I busily check it for the right books and notice Erin closing the sports closet. As she pulls on her blue spring coat, her softball glove rests perfectly wedged between her legs. Today she will pitch in practice after school. I love to watch her pitch on the school's softball diamond. Her eyes light up with concentration and power each time she delivers. The spring smell of the freshly cut grass and the hot dogs adds to the excitement in the air.

Anyway, my morning ritual of choosing which hat to wear is next on my agenda. Today I need more blue in my wardrobe, so I choose the beret that matches my jacket. It hangs underneath my raincoat so I have to spend a few seconds of precious time placing them on other hooks. This annoys me, as I want to make the bus Tony takes.

Erin is ready and waiting for me on the doorstep, so we skip down the steps to the main road and cross to the other side where the sidewalk provides some protection against the early morning traffic. It is 8:00 A.M. and there are plenty of cars cruising through suburbia to the city of Scranton. The sun, the sounds, the footsteps bring me into reality. I know something will happen today. Something is coming my way. I can feel it!

We cross four streets before reaching the bus stop that will take us to our schools. Erin hums her favorite tune from Shania Twain and takes some steps.

"We're still together
Still going strong.
You're still the one
The one I run to
The one that I belong to.
You're still the one I want for life.
You're still the one.
You're still the one that I love.
The only one I dream of. "

My thoughts drift away to a special feeling in my heart. Then I notice him again, Tony! It all seems to be coming together. These are uncharted waters. Another lesson in love? I hope so.

We get on the bus, greet Mr. Mooney, our bus driver, and find some seats on the right-hand side. Some lines from a song by Stevie Wonder, appear in my head,

"As around the sun the earth knows she's revolv-
and the rosebuds know to bloom in early May
just as hate knows love's the cure
you can rest your mind assured that
I'll be loving you always."

The bus drops off Erin first. At the next stop Tony
gets on with two of his boisterous friends. They are always in good moods. He walks to the back of the bus,
winking to me as he passes. The boys are too busy to
socialize. I just turn my head and look out the window
at the passing buildings: the florist, the A&P, the tire
shop, the Mobil station, all lined up each and every day.
The only change is the flow of people coming in and
out. I like to read their faces in a split second. Who is
that? Where are they going? What is up?

The school bus pulls into the parking lot, and Mr.
Mooney opens the door to let us out. I head towards the
entrance, and then suddenly I hear my name, "Carolin,
how are you today?" I turn around with a rush of expec-
tation and relief. It is Tony hurrying towards me. This is
it. We walk beside each other into the hallway, and he
asks me if he can come to my audition Friday night. I
had told him about it two days ago, which seem like
eternity, but he finally got back to me. "Sure, I would
enjoy that. It starts at seven o'clock," was my answer, I
think.

"See you there!" Tony's replies as he runs off towards
his homeroom.

Now I have something to look forward to. That
school day passes quickly. My math and history lessons
are uneventful. In the English lesson we write an essay.
I just finish it and turn it in. As soon as I return to my
desk, I grab my books. In an hour I will give a riding
lesson to schoolchildren. The public bus leaves in fifteen
minutes, and I have to be on it. I open the classroom

door and swing my schoolbag around my shoulder. Freedom again. I am out of here! The wide steps down to the first floor remind me of other days I left the school in relief. When I get outside, the fresh air, the soothing wind, and the warmth of the sun stream towards me. It brings me to my senses, and I dash towards the bus station. I love April.

I sit on the bus watching each building roll by in order — the Medical Arts Building, the Amoco station, and the Sonoco Station before the bridge. My thoughts start drifting away:

This after-school job in Chinchilla helps me make enough money to finance my dance lessons and some clothes. Last night my mother explained one of her ideas about life. That was weird. It turns out she is convinced that we have a number of lives on earth. She told me that we appear at birth with no memory of our previous lives and only later on do our memories begin to surface. She likens the Self to a person who puts on new clothes. In order to dress in new clothes, the Self has to take off the old ones. For example, the new clothes I put on during this lifetime are my personality, my experiences, and my body. According to her, my original Self eventually becomes a force in my personality. The new clothes in this lifetime bring changes that are not necessarily positive. Some of the changes in the personality may be negative. Whether her philosophy is true or not, I don't know. I like to keep my possibilities open.

I pull out of my reflections just before the bus stops on the corner where I usually get off. What really makes me happy today is Tony. He is really interested in attending my audition at the Masonic Temple tomorrow night! What do I really like about him? Hard to say. The feeling is like jumping into a stream on a hot summer afternoon and cooling off! Then you swim ashore and stretch out on the hot rocks leaving the sun to dry you off. A refreshing feeling? For sure!

The bus stops, and I walk home to pick up my mother's car and head for the stables. Driving up Route 6 west, I start feeling great. The radio is blaring. The sun is shining. A wave of good feelings hits me as I take the familiar curves full speed through the notch only to slow down to 45 mph before the body shop on the right hand side of the road—a favorite speed trap for the local police.

When I pull into the driveway leading up to the main house, the row of cars gives me a funny feeling in my stomach. Who is here? There are always surprises at the farm. Anyway, I park my car and walk around the corner of the house to the barn where some kids are waiting for me.

We spend a good deal of time saddling our horses. This afternoon my class and I ride along the river in the mountains west of the Lackawanna Valley. I know about a waterfall with a cliff that many people jump off. My riders are good enough to go that far today. We follow the river north for half an hour.

Just as we were told, beyond the large maples we approach a pool of water with the miniature waterfall and tie the horses to the trees. As we walk up to the rocky surface stepping carefully, the kids get closer and closer to the edge where we all pause for a deep breath. From this perch, it looks much higher than expected. There is no doubt in my mind. I just want to jump! The feeling of rushing full speed at the water below urges me on. The split second experience of being in the air is such a kick. And splashing into the ice cold water is thrilling and refreshing!

I tell the kids that only I am allowed to jump. They can come back sometime with their parents if they want to. It isn't that dangerous, but you never know with thirteen-year-olds. Then I look over the crevasse at the bubbling surface of my destination and ask myself if I really want to do this? I slowly turn around and walk along the precipice one last time before placing my feet in the right position. This is it. The magical moment to stand quietly before casting yourself off — the moment to hurtle myself up in the air and out upon the water. There is no way back — no time for thought.

Silence.
A deep breath.
I spring off the brink.
In a couple of seconds I hit the surface. The cold water swirling around the pool below the cliff is delicious!

In her diary Carolin openly expresses her personality. We observe a girl with the ability to teach young kids how to ride, to enjoy jumping off cliffs, and to attract the boy she wants to attract. Carolin is too involved in her parents' problems, but at least she can reflect over it and get rid of the troubling mental images of their battles when she chooses to. We are left with the picture of a strong girl well engaged in her daily life.

Sixteen-year-olds often go through a parting of the ways from their friends. They suddenly leave old friends and search for new ones. It is a time for trying on new clothes, creating new scenes, and bringing new people into their lives. They often change both their way of speaking and acting. Self-confidence and self-esteem become major issues for teens that are starting to understand new sides of their personality. Sympathies and antipathies take on new meaning, as they are felt more strongly and, therefore, determine more of the teen's actions. At times, middle adolescents insult their scapegoats and are unfair to their best friends. Hate is closer to the surface than it was in their childhood. They misunderstand the situation they are in, time and time again. For many, endless quarrels fill their homes. All of this is part of the chaos and beauty of the middle adolescent years.

In addition, a new awareness of consciousness arises. At first, teens observe everyday consciousness in themselves and their friends. They discover how they behave and how others behave as well. They see the patterns of thought in people around them. And with the help of media experiences they study human behavior from a distance. Everything from the news to soap operas is studied by the curious minds of our mid-teenagers. What puzzles them most are the mental images and feelings coming to them from their subconscious. These are powerful and sometimes disconcerting. One such memory from the subconscious is expressed in Carolin's diary. As she ran up the stairs, the images in her memory of her parents quarrelling reappeared. The picture images release feelings of pain that she deals with in a split second. She does not ignore them. She sees the images clearly and is then totally fed up with them. By the time she brushed her teeth, she pulls out of the pain completely!

Subconscious images may also be beautiful and amazing. Carolin touched some of hers in a brief moment when she compared the feeling of her boyfriend with drying off on a hot rock in the summer sun. Some teens struggle to fathom the wealth of their subconscious experiences by following their dreams and searching for knowledge. Most teens strive to integrate their personality in their everyday consciousness. Because the personality has so much power and feeling, these teens are often intense, though immature emotionally. They easily lose perspective and are unpredictable in their behavior, but they are robust. Once the personality blossoms, the purpose of suffering is seen, idealism is ignited, and they start thinking about life and death differently. All of these sides of life become awesome mysteries with which they start to grapple.

Late Adolescence

The third phase begins when the teenager's Self emerges. Some of the first signs may be observed in the eighteenth year. The teen is often convinced of his invincibility! No one can touch his power. Surprisingly enough, this attitude appears just at the time when goals and impulses for the future are no longer a vague curiosity, but now are seen as commitments. The teenager feels committed to create the life he needs to live. He knows that it is up to him to get what he wants out of life. His ideals develop as a clear reflection of his youthful individuality. Grasping his own ideals and creating his own future may be the greatest responsibility he receives as a teen.

We can observe our teens not only in their new maturity but also in their increased insecurity. The nineteen-year-old is light years away from the person he was as a thirteen-year-old! When teens look back at their experiences since thirteen, they may remember the radical changes they went through in their body shape and hormone activity. One day they were calm, and the next day they were filled with moodiness, anxiety, and secrecy. During their early teenage years they have walked the gauntlet of self-criticism, spent years being extremely pre-occupied with themselves and repeatedly insecure. They may see their new independence as well as their peer-validated experiences. The whole question of normal-abnormal was painfully reviewed from many sides. An even stronger issue was the battle between maturity and immaturity they fought out. Only they could find the right answer. The same was true of their sexual lives and their partying. As kids they were often unconcerned about taking drugs, smoking, and drinking. They were not worried about risky behavior. Experimentation led to choice and consistency.

The nineteen-year-old also looks to the future. One very clear sign of the passing of the teenage years appears around the age of twenty, when the individual takes a radical new step as an individual freeing himself from the influences of family, nationality, education, and society.

The Self emerges into the world in a new way during the process of individuation. At this time the teen learns to stand on his own two feet. And he goes out into the world to find the people who can teach him something.

At this time the Self participates in a two-fold process. It not only becomes independent, but it has to be found anew — directly in relation to the hard won experiences of this lifetime. Daily life can be fragmented because his life is filled with new strength and complete vulnerability. The teen experiences himself split between security and insecurity while he achieves independence from outside influences as well as creates a new integration of the Self in this lifetime. For each individual this process is unique. By taking off our blinders and turning in new directions towards our teens, we can practice observing these exciting moments in their lives. We can also start seeing some of the idealism in their motives for action and the newborn wisdom in their words.

As you see in Fig. 9, the Self in late adolescence no longer lingers below the surface. It has emerged into the center of the flower where it works with the cognitive profile. The relationship between the Self and the other key factors has changed radically. Now it is strong enough to begin the process of integration into the experiences with the key factors in this lifetime and also the liberation from some of the effects of the experiences. Chapter 11 is devoted to this theme. When the Self emerges, teens grow up, and they become more mature and independent.

Late Adolescence
(Ages 18–20)

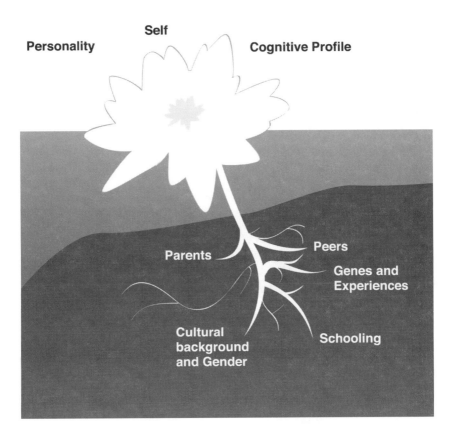

Self

Personality

Cognitive Profile

Parents

Peers

Genes and Experiences

Cultural background and Gender

Schooling

Fig. 9

CHAPTER 9

Another Heart

I speak with many teens that experience their Self. It is always an amazing moment for them. Some of them know the importance of their experiences. Others are unsure, especially if the adults in their lives are not supportive. I know many kids with parents who, for one reason or another, deny the Self. These teens often have a long and difficult path to follow before they can integrate their experiences. They have to search for mentors who can acknowledge the significance of their experiences and then guide them through the integration process. By integration all I mean is bringing the newfound power of the Self into their daily life in a healthy way.

The integration takes place in the personality that is centered in the "other heart" region of the teen. I call this the "other heart" merely because it works from the physical heart but is not limited to physical properties. The "other heart" is the center of the human being—a non-physical region of activity where the personality and the core of the personality are active. We cannot see the "other heart," just as we cannot see the personality. But we can sense it. We can feel it, and we can use our intelligences to work with it.

Carolin is an example of a teen with the great advantage of one supportive parent, her mother. She does not need to go through a long search for the acknowledgement of her Self. In addition to her mother, she also confides in me. I became Carolin's mentor in the moment she told me about her unexpected experience on the beach. I listened to her with great attention that afternoon, not only because she was so eager to talk, but also because she convinced me of the truth of her experience. She was searching for validation.

I have reconstructed our conversation to give you a feeling for the experience. Carolin and I sat in my living room. She begins:

> I have something to tell you! I want to talk about a discovery I made this week. I know it is true, even if I cannot prove it to anyone else. It is a new experience for me, and I wonder what you think about it. On Saturday evening I was walking alone on the beach and into the sand dunes. The sun was setting and I felt peaceful. My thoughts became more and more powerful until I experienced my heart. It was strange and familiar at the same time. I discovered that I not only have a physical heart but another, more profound heart. I experienced it and now I know it is a part of me. Do you know what I am talking about?

I paused for a moment to collect my thoughts. This was a real challenge! Just exactly how far I should go posed an immediate problem. Carolin looked curiously at me. All I could do was throw myself into the exchange.

> I know what you are talking about. It is something I have tried to understand again and again for the last twenty years. When I was twenty years old, I also discovered my "other heart." It happened one afternoon while I was walking along the Charles River in Cambridge. It was a sunny spring day. I sat by the river, closed my eyes, and experienced what I would call my Self.

The whole experience took place in my heart, but I reached far beyond my physical heart. I crossed a threshold.

What you are really talking about is nothing less than the true center of every human being. I believe you experienced your Self entering into your "other heart." It was a discovery. In that moment you met your Self — the core of your personality again. A window was opened for you. Now you can work with that window.

Most teens have experienced glimpses of their heart forces that are not related directly to the physical heart. They come into contact with their heart when they fall in love or when they have deep experiences of nature, by the ocean, in the woods or on the desert. It also can be felt when they have an inner experience of the change of seasons. It appears in a glance and disappears all too quickly. As a result, few teens find ways of developing these experiences consciously. Nowadays the "other heart" is not mainstream knowledge. It is very close to all of us but still far away from our minds, unless we choose to take it seriously.

"For me it is so obvious," Carolin replied. "It was a new experience but strangely familiar. When I mentioned it to a guy I met on the beach the next day, he did not understand it at all. It made him uncomfortable. He told me to be careful. Then I realized that I could not go any further with the conversation."

We both sit silently, reflecting over our thoughts.

"I think children see it much more clearly than adults," Carolin continued boldly. "My younger sister is very strong — much stronger than I am, and she sees much more than I do. Her age group has its own power of vision. They see right through us, even though we are older than they are. You can not fool them either."

It seemed natural to go into some depth now that she had raised the issue. Her maturity made me forget how young she was. Age was no longer a barrier between us. "When you approach the center of a human being in the heart region, you enter sacred ground. Teenagers are in the phase of life in which they develop this region independently. That is one of the main reasons why you are going through such indescribable changes. Because your inner feelings are now exposed to the world, you become vulnerable. Your private life is turned inside out. Your adolescence years are then marked by the fact that new heart experiences are entering your life. It takes time for you to get to know yourself again. You have probably noticed how awkward, helpless, and strange your classmates have become during the last two years. It is not easy for them to be constantly cool and together!

"No two people are alike because each adolescent receives his or her unique, spiritual heart in the teenage years. You have experienced a moment of that development. In many cultures the fact that teenagers have matured and become responsible for their actions is celebrated in rituals or confirmation. What has been protected by the wonders of childhood breaks into the teenager's daily life. A new relationship between the Self and the world unfolds. From this moment on, whatever you do in the outside world is also experienced deep inside the 'other heart.' Your Self is emerging into your heart. This will continue for a couple of years. Orientation is essential, but difficult at first.

"You can learn a lot from biographies of people who were in contact with their Self. One great example is Dr. Martin Luther King Jr. I can tell you about one episode from his thirty-sixth year that illustrates how he could act from his heart.

"No one on the earth could help Dr. King. He was out on the edge of violence all alone, and the whole nation was watching. What would he do? His aides had called him from the Brown Chapel parsonage on Sunday afternoon, March 7, 1965. In the background he could hear the moaning and groaning of his wounded friends. Five hundred and fifty supporters had crossed the bridge on Highway 80 carrying bedrolls and blankets, only to be met by the Alabama highway patrol standing three deep, across four lanes, wearing gas masks, blue hard hats, and wielding billy clubs.

"The entire Civil Rights Movement was on the line. How could they carry out the march to Montgomery against such odds? If they tried to cross the bridge, only more bloodshed would await them. Should he go in for a compromise? Should he retreat? Should he confront the police?

"Only he could find the next step. It would have to arise in his consciousness as an intuition that would be strong enough and realistic enough to be put into action on Tuesday. Sometime between Sunday and Monday afternoon an idea appeared to him. He could trust it, for it was one with which Dr. King could unite himself. The next step was to act from the heart.

"He sent telegram messages to religious leaders all over the country. They were asked to come to Selma for the march to Montgomery on Tuesday. Four hundred rabbis, priests, ministers, nuns, students, and lay leaders responded to the appeal.

"But on Tuesday they were met with a federal court order banning the march. From Washington, leaders phoned to ask them not to march. There was no way back now. The intuition had to be proven in reality. So he addressed 1,500 marchers at Brown Chapel on Tuesday and told them he had decided to defy the court restriction. Two abreast, he led them to Pettis Bridge, where a U.S. marshal read the restraining orders. The marchers stopped for a prayer in front of the highway patrol. Then they turned around and went back to town. On that day, Dr. King acted from his heart. See what I mean?"

Carolin just nodded. Many ideas had certainly crossed her mind while I was trying to expand upon the theme. As usual, she had a bundle of her own thoughts to share.

"I discovered my 'other heart' in a split moment. It was suddenly there and I saw it. I felt it. Later on in the day it happened again. I am glad to know that you have also seen it and that you have tried to understand it again and again. Every day I see adults who are living such limited lives. Their faces show a lot of pain. They say one thing and do another. I can't believe how limited their thoughts are. Our neighbor is a grown-up man, but he has the stupidest hang-ups. He gets upset about the most ridiculous things. I feel sorry for people like that. But there is no way I can help them. Do you think he has chosen to be so limited?"

I continued eagerly, "If you do not take your 'other heart' seriously, no one else will. It will not be developed. And you will not be connected to it. You will continue to say one thing and do something else for the rest of your life. It is that simple. As I said, the Self that you have experienced in a brief moment on the shore is centered in the 'other heart.' It is not only the center of the human being, but the field upon which moral actions are played out. If you can learn to act out of your heart, then you will say one thing and do the same. Your Self will create a healthy connection with your personality. You take part in what you think and what you do. When you have become one with your deeds, each action will strengthen your moral life. Not until you think and act out of your heart do you integrate what you know with what you do. All intellectual activity is merely a starting point. It needs to become one with your deeds. So every teen has a long path to travel. No one is perfect. What is most important is to learn from your experiences."

Carolin had no further comments. She is a special girl with a lot of wisdom and a high level of thinking at the early age of eighteen. She deserves whatever advice I can offer. I decide to finish the conversation by giving her some ways of focusing on her Self in the "other heart" region.

"Now that you have experienced your Self in a brief moment, you will need to focus on that part of your life again and again. The goal is to make the Self a healthy part of your personality and your everyday life. It is vulnerable in the sense that only you can work with it. It is easy to lose your focus when all the power of your passions, your intelligence, and your habits overpower you. I know many teens who are able to focus on their Self again and again while also developing other sides of their personality. You can't hide away in a cloister or any other protected environment. Martin Luther King, Jr. did not hide away. He entered into the issues facing his family, his friends, his parish, his town, his county, his state, and his country.

"Teens like you are less protected than they were in the past. The advantage is that you have so many possibilities for developing yourself and the responsibility is left to you. You need to work, to socialize and live your life like anyone else. The difficulties lie in the loneliness and the continual hard work that needs to take place to grasp your cognitive profile and create you own path of development.

"A good place to begin is with your concentration. Now that you have had such a powerful meeting with your Self, try to keep it as a window to the greatest resource you have in your life. Develop your devotion to that gift. Now that you have received it, try to discover it in others so they also may find it. Your cognitive profile is enormous. We can talk about this the next time we meet. All I can say today is that your senses and your intelligence can be grasped by the power of your Self and used in your daily life in a healthy way. The key is to focus on the Self in your 'other heart' during the day whether you are with people or alone. I do this each day in a number of ways. I create an inner dialogue with my Self by writing down new ideas that cross my mind. I close my eyes and sink my attention into my heart region. I ask myself questions silently when I meet people in order to get a feeling for where they are coming from. And I go for walks in nature to clear out my head and listen to my heart. All of these habits of mine are ways of focusing. You can find your own way of doing this. It is a lot of fun!

"You clearly have a strong relationship to nature. One other way of developing your concentration is to go out to a lake or mountain regularly and practice listening to the sounds around you. Observe a plant and close you eyes afterwards to build your own inner picture of the plant. Go into all of the details you can remember and imagine. Build a picture in your memory. Then open your eyes again and correct your picture. When you relax, looking at the plant, try to observe new details. Then repeat the process in your memory. You make a new inner picture. This will sharpen your ability to observe nature. You can use the same ability to observe people and develop your art in New York this fall at Parsons. I do this a lot at my favorite lake. It helps me focus on nature, and it puts me in touch with the core of my personality. Simple stuff, but powerful!"

CHAPTER 10

Speak for Yourself

It is easy to forget how much resistance is involved whenever a teen speaks for herself. We all have substantial lags between our thoughts and our actions that need to be overcome each time we speak for ourselves. The more teens try, the harder it gets. This is due to the fact that each teen needs to break through layers of superficiality to reach the depth inside where they create their own thoughts and actions. Speaking for yourself demands continual effort. It can never be automatic.

Breaking through the Superficiality

Speaking for herself comes much easier for Carolin than for Jason. She does so regularly, while he almost never speaks for himself. This is because she is less superficial than he is. Throughout childhood and at school Jason has always received answers to the questions he asks. His attitude is that being told the right answers is more important than asking the right questions. However, life is not that easy. There are no final answers to most of the real questions being asked. Anyone with all of the right answers and judgments is bound to be very superficial in his experience of the world.

Jason has not yet learned how to concentrate over a long period of time. He seldom experiences a logical progression from one thought to another at school or at home. In order to master the daily stress, he quickly processes facts in the form of conclusions. And one copied conclusion after the other is then memorized at school, spit out on tests, and often forgotten. This is one reason why he is tired of school, and he has lost interest in subjects such as history and chemistry. Due to this superficial way of learning, Jason's ability to create new concepts remains weak. He merely repeats what others have taught him. For example, in middle and high school mathematics Jason memorized formulas and solved problems rather than learning the concept behind the formula. This method is very effective for some kids, but Jason fell behind when he could not engage in the memorization at the rate set by the teacher.

Every Conclusion Counts

Most kids sleep in their heavily equipped media centers. All day long they have televisions, computers, and music machines playing full blast. In addition to schoolwork and occasional reading, all of these sounds and pictures are processed as a part of their daily conclusions. But unless the teen puts his conclusions in a meaningful relationship, the conclusions remain chaotic. Why are Jason's conclusions chaotic? — simply because he has not made sense of the pictures, sounds, and the knowledge that he has accumulated that day. Jason seldom reflects over his conclusions.

We can compare Jason's daily process of cognition to the evening news! First, there are five quick advertisements before the forty-second shots from the catastrophe in Indonesia are shown. Then he is whisked off to Northern Canada for fifty seconds of land disputes before the latest murder trial in the states is commented on in 25 seconds. Powerful pictures and simple conclusions accompany each shot. The teenager has impressions from three parts of the world with no possibility of making an individual judgment on the real issues at stake. He is left with nothing more than superficial conclusions. The passive attitude becomes a habit.

My experience is that every conclusion absorbed during the course of a life continues to work in the teenager's consciousness as unrelated images that reappear instinctively. The conclusions are not passive, and they do not disappear even if they are forgotten. The problem for Jason is that he has not been able to work on his conclusions and develop individual judgments and concepts that are put into a meaningful relationship. The mass of unrelated information weakens his will to concentrate. Instead of active concentration over a longer period of time with critical analysis from a variety of viewpoints, Jason indulges in an unconscious habit of consuming mental images that are already conclusions. Nothing more! The most devastating part of this aspect of teenage development today is that the conclusions become habit forming. The habit, in a way, craves more conclusions — more powerful pictures to consume. His habit of passive consumption replaces his inner capacity to concentrate and analyze.

Emptiness in Abundance

I am convinced that the emptiness millions of teenagers feel despite their hours of entertainment is due to the superficiality of their experience. There remains a total lack of content in the teen. This emptiness is not passive. It works on the inside of the personality like a volcano, and no one can reach it except the individual teenager. The passive teenager becomes not only aggressive but temporarily stupid. This is one reason why we see so many insensitive and apathetic teens. They have not yet learned how to integrate their superficial media-experiences and their chaotic conclusions into the ability of speaking for themselves.

Teens Need to Explode!

No one likes to be manipulated. No one likes to be superficial. When teenagers discover how superficial their lives are, they either submit to a negative picture of themselves, or they explode in outrage! The initial explosion may be directed to the outside world, or it may be directed inwardly in the form of self-destructive activities. Becoming outraged is important. They need to explode! We can only hope that the explosion does not become self-destructive. Whenever teenagers are outraged about injustice, lameness, and emptiness, they begin a search for true integrity. Their passion for freedom and change is ignited. The teenager is mad at that which represses.

When teens discover a blockade, the reaction is strong. This is a new step forward in their willpower. The challenge for every teen is to handle the newly released forces of will so they can move in a positive direction. Teenage anger is a very positive force that is essential to strengthen their will to tear down personal and social blockades. It needs to be worked on. Throughout their entire life anger may be transformed into real love for other people and interest in the world.

On the Thinking Edge

As you noticed in her diary, Carolin is now striving for integrity and freedom. She lives with the expectations from her family, peers, and society, while struggling to define her own life in line with her passions and goals. On the outside Carolin looks like the perfect teen—a good girl. But she is much more radical than most people notice. Now that she has experienced her Self, she has a new understanding of who she is today. But she also sees a large discrepancy between who she is and who she wants to become. This gap is hard for her to bear.

Like so many other teens, Carolin has a strong willpower. This helps her in two stages of the process of speaking for herself:

Stage 1 – The Thinking Stage. I describe this stage in three steps.
Stage 2 – The Action Stage. This takes only one step!

Stage 1 – The Thinking Stage

Figure 10 gives us a picture of the thinking stage. It has three steps. Without developing her ability to think, Carolin will never be able to make her own decisions and learn to speak for herself. She needs to concentrate for long periods of time and follow all three steps in the thinking process from *conclusion* to *multiple judgments* and then on to the *creation of concepts*.

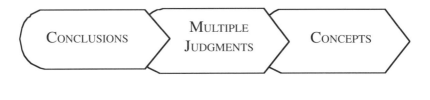

CONCLUSIONS   MULTIPLE JUDGMENTS   CONCEPTS

Fig. 10

Stage 2 – The Action Stage

The second stage is to bring the power of her thinking into her actions. In the action stage, she not only creates new concepts, but she acts on them. She does what she decides to do. It sounds easy, but it is very powerful. Many teens never get that far because they drown in their habits of passively consuming conclusions, or they get stuck in concepts they have learned from other people. We see the latter clearly in countries run by dictators or ideological parties where ministers of education and indoctrination see to it that kids are never taught how to create their own concepts. They accomplish the manipulation by forcing kids to continually repeat the chosen concepts. Teens drown in dogmas and ideologies, except for those who fight back, of course!

Attitudes

In order to speak for yourself, a teen needs to go to the depth of her personality where her attitudes are found. The most important attitude to establish while learning to speak for yourself is to be willing to start all over again. I mean again and again and again! This can be fun! In her early adolescence Samantha loved repeating the slalom course she tore through. She learned to speak for herself on skis. The training strengthened her willpower and reinforced her good attitude. Each new effort strengthened the relationship between her thinking and her will power. When both stages of thinking and acting are carried through, a teen takes part in the motives for her actions. She speaks for herself.

Jimmy had a larger gap between his thinking and his willpower than Samantha. He was unsure of himself in group settings, so he was usually looking for trouble. It was hard for him to close the gap between what he thought and what he did! But once he stepped into a sailboat, he was totally concentrated and confident. He could consistently repeat his efforts in sailing and learn from his mistakes. In a sailboat that came easy for him.

It takes a strong will to develop the art of speaking for yourself over many years. But no one needs to be perfect. Everyone will make mistakes. That is the beauty of experience. It teaches.

A major step forward is taken when a teen observes the conclusions she makes. The old conclusions appear, and with the power of her thinking she strives for new conclusions. Martin Seligman, a psychologist at the University of Pennsylvania, recognizes this importance of observing your conclusions. For the following reasons, he built this cognitive ability into the Penn Prevention Program:

> We aimed to teach children that thoughts are verifiable and changeable, that they do not need to believe the first thought that pops into their head; "automatic thoughts," which we all have, occur just on the edge of awareness. They are the fleeting, barely perceptible statements that we say to ourselves throughout the day. Although such thoughts are fast, and, thus, hard to detect, they directly bring about sadness, anxiety, and anger.

Our first step, then, was to teach children to monitor the things that they say to themselves.

Once children can capture their automatic thoughts, they need to learn how to evaluate their accuracy. Judging the accuracy of accusations is a skill that most children already have, but they do not use it when the accusations issue from inside. When accused of being lazy or selfish or boorish by, say a friend, most children and adults will counter criticism by rattling off a list of concrete examples that prove it false. Usually, however, we do not use this skill when we hurl the accusation at ourselves. [4]

If Jason could learn to observe his "automatic thoughts" as Seligman calls these conclusions, he would start out on a very productive process of raising his awareness. Unfortunately though, Jason is not able to observe his conclusions. No one has taught him how. He still accepts everything as facts. For example, he does not observe his self-critical thoughts from a distance and then search for alternatives. They remain mental images that come up repeatedly in situations. This happens to him when he reads the paper or magazines. He automatically judges himself as less valuable than the stars he reads about. It has now reached the point where he consciously tries to avoid situations where his self-critical thoughts automatically pop up and make him unhappy. Avoidance reinforces his emotional isolation.

Now we can approach the method I use to help teens strengthen their ability to think. I take them down the path from *conclusion* to *judgments* and then to individual *concepts*. These steps build self-esteem and flexibility. Let us exam all three steps mentioned in Stage 1 — the Thinking Stage.

Step 1 — Carolin Forms Conclusions

Forming conclusions is the first step. As I mentioned earlier in this chapter, we continuously form conclusions in our daily lives, in our media experiences, and in our cognition. For example, on a superficial level Carolin may conclude that it is Monday, that school starts at 8.30 A.M., and that the weather is stormy. These are everyday conclusions.

As her mentor I challenge Carolin to work on her conclusions. The area I usually pick with teens who have an experience of their Self is the concept of the Self. I take them through all three steps using the Self as our area of focus. Now I will teach Carolin how to develop her thinking through the three steps and then act on the concept of Self that she has brought forth. This is the most powerful way for her to actively integrate the core of her personality into the key factors of her personality development.

Rather than repeating old mental images of her identity, I teach her to bring forth new conclusions concerning her Self. For example, she can conclude that her Self comes and goes like the rhythms in a song. Sometimes the Self is present and powerful, and other times it is in the background. She can conclude that the Self is part of her personality. She concludes that it is hard to identify and easy to forget. She also has her experiences of her Self that remain in her memory as conclusions.

Carolin is already active in observing the mental images that pop up automatically in her conclusions, and she is clearly searching for alternatives. I reinforce this drive in her. You may have noticed her efforts in her diary when she describes walking up the stairs to get ready for school, and she has a flash of her dream the night before of her parents quarrelling years ago. By the time she brushed her teeth, she is able to shake off the unwanted conclusions. So she is in the first phase of the process as shown in the Fig.11 below.

Fig. 11

Step 2—Carolin Judges her Conclusions

The next step for Carolin is to judge her conclusions. When Carolin places her own judgments on the conclusions, she develops what I like to call *multiple judgments*. The issue at hand is judged from a number of viewpoints. Each teen has a palate of judgments. They can be superficial, cold, egotistical judgments, or they can be part of the teen's search for the truth.

On a deeper level I help Carolin judge her conclusions about her Self. My goal is to guide her into judging the existing conclusions she has about the Self and also into conclusions she has heard from other people. She should ask herself whatever questions she likes. Is the Self for real? Am I kidding myself? Why does it come and go? Or she can make definitive judgements such as:

> My Self is familiar.
> It is a weak experience compared to my body.
> It is a subtle feeling or a clear thought.
> The Self is a non-physical part of me.

As her mentor, I find it always fascinating to hear the individual judgments. She reveals herself in the multiple judgment phase. I try to help her view as many conclusions as possible without getting stuck in certain areas or distracted by other things. The longer she is active in Step 2, the better!

MULTIPLE
JUDGMENTS

Fig. 12

Step 3 — Carolin Creates Original Concepts

The third step is taken when she puts both her conclusions and her multi-dimensional judgments into a meaningful relationship. I call this *concept-creativity*. When Carolin creates original concepts, all of her multiple judgments are brought together in a new synthesis. For example in Carolin's concept creativity concerning the Self, she judges the Self in contrast to her body, in relation to her personality, and as a part of her daily life. The new concept is hers. Teens do not express their concepts easily. In my conversations with teens I always notice a lot of resistance when we come into the concept phase. This is largely due to the fact that the concepts are personal and not easily expressed in words. It is hard work. Sometimes drawings help. I usually know that new concepts have been created when I talk with them about the subject. When they are able to dwell on the subject for a longer period of time and bring forth important relationships, then I know they have done the work necessary to create original concepts. This process gives the teen maturity and self-confidence. They know that they know.

Carolin has the passionate need to speak for herself. She wants inner freedom and conviction in order to carry on her life despite the problems she has from her past. She strives for a new relationship between her thinking and her actions. And I have pointed out to her that this must take place in her "other heart." To speak for herself at the age of eighteen, Carolin must observe her conclusions, judge them from as many angles as possible, and then create new concepts. In time, this will lead to her individual concept of Self. Once she has created her original concept of Self, a major part of her integration process will be underway. As her mentor I will continuously appeal to her using her cognitive profile to create new concepts in as many areas as she likes. I use this three-phased method to help teens gain security, because it respects their inner freedom. They do the work, not the mentor!

By practicing the creation of individual concepts, Carolin not only gains the confidence to know where she stands, but she gains the ability to change. This strengthens her relationship to her Self. In the future she can create many new concepts, all depending on what she is working on. Do not underestimate how powerful this ability is for her. It brings her thinking to the edge. In this way her Self drives her personality to new experiences.

Carolin dwells in the third phase as expressed in the following Fig. 13.

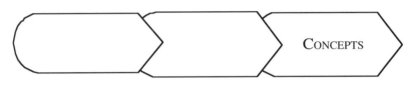

CONCEPTS

Fig. 13

Step 2—The Action Stage Builds Teenage Confidence

The creation of individual concepts is an invaluable source of confidence—one that gives the teen personal strength for a whole lifetime. This happens when the teen acts on her original concepts! She not only thinks—she acts! If you pay attention you will see how your teen acts on her new concepts. She may speak for herself or take new initiatives!

Teens know that they know the subjects they are mastering at school, the sports they are playing, or the trade, handicraft or technology they are learning. Their concept-creativity lets them know where they stand. The less confident they are about their knowledge, the more insecure and restless they become. As soon as your teen discovers that she is good in an area, you know she is headed in the right direction.

I have used the two-stage method of concept creativity with groups of teens in the classroom. This method is valuable no matter what subject you teach. The method is to dive into interesting pictures of real life situations that express extreme polarities every teenager has already experienced—such as love and hate or freedom and repression. The goal is to give the teenagers the opportunity to create their own conclusions and judgments and in the end develop their own concepts. When teens are able to create their own concepts through analytical thinking, they become more gifted in creating new concepts in the future. And they learn to act on them!

CHAPTER 11

Cross-currents

In this chapter we step far into the personality where teens are engulfed in two powerful processes. The first process is one of expansion towards freedom. They make huge efforts to become free, to break out of their limitations, and lead lives they want to live. Teens passionately want to change. This means leaving experiences with their key factors behind and creating new relationships, new skills, and new values.

The other process entails integrating the Self into the key factors in a healthy way. Integration takes place when teens try to create meaningful relationships with their parents, their peers, and their cultural background, ans well as put past experiences in their proper place.

Because these processes work in opposite directions, but belong together as mutually enriching factors in personality development, I call them cross-currents. The innovation teens muster to create breakthroughs in their cross-currents is carried out by their Self. Innovation is possible when the Self engages in the cognitive profile to slowly activate and transform a small part of their personality. Each action in the cross-current process takes place on the edge. Here teens need constructive adults who can guide them along the way. In this chapter we will see how Carolin is already making significant steps in her cross-current processes.

Continue the dialogue!

With constructive dialogues we can help teens dive into the integration process or support them in liberating themselves from influences from the past. Teens need to clarify their values, find their purpose, and distinguish between reality and fantasy. They need to resolve internal conflicts and put harsh events into perspective. Many teens search for a healthy perspective on their situation so they can stop internalizing other people's problems. Many of the adults I know shy away from helping their teens integrate the power of the Self, often because the adults have not done enough of this work themselves.

It is not as difficult as we imagine. If your teen trusts you, then get involved in the cross-currents and help them swim in the direction of their choice.

As we head out into this heavy sea, you should be asking yourself the following questions:

"Which part of the cross-current process is my teen most involved in at this time, the liberation stream or the integration stream?"

"From what exactly does my teen want to be liberated?"

"Which key factors is he or she integrating?"

By asking yourself these questions and answering them as honestly as possible, you have a realistic basis to work from. In this chapter I will share with you exactly how I would work with Jason and Carolin. And keep in mind your teen as you read!

Before we go zooming off into the cross-currents, I want to give you a valuable perspective when dealing with conflicts or complicated personal issues. In the last chapter of his book *Leadership Without Easy Answers*, Ronald A. Heifetz of Harvard University offers simple, but constructive ways in which we can help people focus on their conflicts. In my opinion, his work with adults is also valid for late adolescents. Heifitz helps people externalize the conflict by distinguishing between the role they are playing and themselves. He challenges the individual to give the conflict back to its rightful owner. Heifitz calls this important ability "getting to the balcony"! With that he means not merely being carried away while dancing on the floor but mentally moving your focus up to the balcony so you can look down on the dance floor with greater perspective.

"If one can get to the balcony instead of getting caught up in recreating the problem internally, one can seize the opportunity of the case in point for identifying the challenges and inventing options for action." [5]

The adult, whether a mentor, a parent or a teacher, can reinforce the teen's striving for liberation or integration by keeping his or her attention where it belongs. As Heifetz rightfully points out, personalizing the issue most often produces work avoidance and shifts the responsibility to the wrong person. This is very prevalent among teens! Very often teens over-personalize their issues and distort what they hear. They tune out and lose direction.

In the following pages from Jason's diary, you will recognize that he desperately needs to get to the balcony and preserve his purpose in life. He is internalizing the unhealthy attitudes and thoughts from his past years. The boy is struggling with the tragic loss of Cindy. Reverence for life is slowly fading from his horizon. He has not found his Self, and he remains a captive of his own little personality. Jason tells the story of the fall of his freshman year at Penn State. If he doesn't obtain new perspectives, I am afraid he will drown in a spiral of self-destructive actions.

I just came back to my dorm after the professional wrestling event at the Bryce Jordan Center. Unbelievable! Is that entertainment? The mentality scares me! I mean adults are screaming their heads off. Eight thousand kids are sitting next to them with popcorn boxes and huge cups of coke. The smell of this place makes my stomach do back flips! The brutality, the swearing, and the cheating are carrying daddies away. Talk about stupidity. At least the kids get the action live. Flesh and blood is better than Saturday morning TV violence. Great family role models in the ring.

The pair event was pretty heavy. First they knocked one guy unconscious and threw him out of the ring. Then they started kicking the other guy everywhere you can imagine. So he is thrown out of the ring on his back and can't get up. Which is a good time for the other guy to jump on top of him and hold him down while his partner climbs up on the posts to get a flying jump on the guy's head. People get off on the groaning. At least it shows that the victim is still human and still alive! Neanderthal communication. After the show they interviewed the winners. One guy said he liked our capital building in Harrisburg so much that he is saving some of his prize money to run for Governor.

Two weeks before Christmas the Dalai Lama will come to the center to speak about "Healing Anger." I am looking forward to that. Pennsylvania, the state of contrasts!

I walk back to my room and put on my father's Band of Gypsies album where Hendrix plays a thing called, "Machine Gun." I listen to it full blast three times in a row. Shit, that guy could get his message across, "Evil man make me kill you. Evil man make you kill me. Evil man make me kill you, even though we're only…" Then I go to brush my teeth. Next to the mirror on the bathroom wall I read my favorite poem before I go to sleep.

We Wear Sunglasses

Are we the last
To walk by the waterfalls in February
And feel your warmth?

To wear our sunglasses
On a dreary, rainy afternoon?
To get lost in time
Discussing daydreams?

Are we alone
To hear the music
When the tune has long been done?
To feel the magic of curiosity
Alive within our souls?
To take a trip merely for
The sake of the journey?

Can we exist
In a time where polyester
Is socially unacceptable?
In a place where shades of gray
Exist only within the smog?
In a world where no one owns sunglasses
And waterfalls never melt?

— Stephanie Morgan[6]

'In a world where no one owns sunglasses
And waterfalls never melt?'

How many times have I read that poem since I cut it out of the Calliope, the Abington Heights High School's literary club magazine? Why do I still have it on my wall? Don't ask me. But Stephanie is a girl to remember. Anyway, it is already November. Here I stand brushing my teeth on my way to bed after an uneventful night. What am I up to? I guess I am trying to enjoy my general studies before I go into the undergraduate program for computer sciences. My goal is to be on the cutting edge of ecommerce in five years. Not a bad goal. Shall I do that or what?

Summer seems like ages ago. Yesterday afternoon I went down to watch the football team practice. Those guys are running their asses off! You could drive a truck through some of those holes. I am talking about great blockers. And the starting quarterback is a magician with the ball. That is what I call high-level sports. The Lions are having a heck of a year. We'll see how they tackle Michigan State next week!

We partied last Saturday until dawn. It was part of the initiation to the club I have been asked to join. Not too bad at all. They deprive you of sleep, food, and showers for two days to see if you can be one of the guys. The drinking is outrageous. I have seen drinking games, but this is beyond my imagination. It doesn't really matter to me whether I join or not.

Actually, nothing really matters after I lost Cindy three months ago in a car accident. I keep hearing my mother's voice on the phone telling me that she is in the emergency room at the Moses Taylor, and they don't expect her to live. I still see her car rolling over and over into the guard-rail. Oh God! She was my best friend. I really loved her. I know I will never love anyone again. I felt that at her funeral at Hickory Grove. That is it for me. My heart is locked up. Someone has taken the key and thrown it away.

I study long hours to get my mind off the pain. It still hurts to see people cuddling up or walking hand in hand. I am really tired and dizzy after the Calculus course. It is hard to concentrate. But right after Christmas we have four major exams. I still have two papers to write. They really hit you with an information overload!

Some of these graduate students are spineless wonders. They can't handle it, if I question their comments on my papers. You would think they were way beyond the rest of us! Arrogant bookworms! Have you ever seen a bookworm? One of those nightcrawlers that got lost in the library five years ago? I have. After it has rained, you walk all over the fourth floor with a flashlight in order to take them by surprise. That is when they hang out in the moist grass—soaking in the darkness. Then you jump on them before they can coil back into their books! We used to catch them in Clarks Summit and go fishing. Here they correct undergraduate papers.

As Laura said on the phone during my birthday call, I am getting cynical. I admit it. You know how it works. They pull up to your house and tell you to get in. Before you know it the guys in the white jackets are telling you what to do and how to speak. Brainwash city! Just kidding. I am not really cynical. I am as standardized as everyone else. That is why I stand out. I am one of the guys everyone wants. They all want us in America: the political parties, the churches, the sects, the advertising agencies, Uncle Sam, you name it. They want me. All I have to do is follow their leads, take on their value structure and attitudes. They know who I want to be and how I want to live. They have it all: my music, my style, and my future. I am flexible, charming, and aggressive.

At the age of nineteen Jason is turning cynical and cold. You can detect in Jason's cynicism that he needs to break away from his family and his cultural background in Pennsylvania to become independent. The cynicism indicates that Jason has not engaged his cognitive profile sufficiently to liberate himself from those key factors. He also needs engage his cognitive profile to integrate into the same factors in a healthy way. This is not easy for someone with a "poor me attitude." His biggest disappointment is no longer his chaotic father but now the loss of Cindy, which has totally devastated him. He is also in danger of closing off his heart and never tapping into his Self. Jason really needs to get up on the "balcony" so he can actively engage in both cross-current processes. To do this he needs guidance.

As I wrote earlier, the cross-current processes integrate the Self into the key factors of the personality while also liberating the Self from the affects of past experiences. Once again the goal is to bring as much power of the Self as possible into this process in the personality. Integration and liberation are fancy words for everyday processes! Yet simple things are often the most powerful.

Here is a picture of the cross-current processes of integration and liberation.

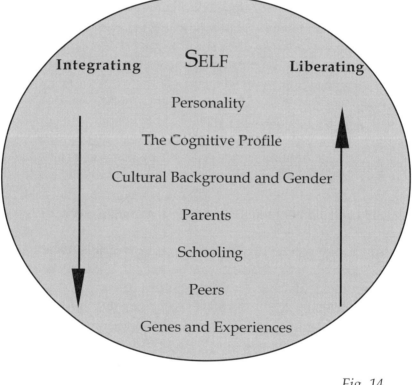

Fig. 14

Every movement in the cross-currents follows the individual's timing. I have seen teens with the maturity Carolin demonstrates begin this process as early as their sixteenth year. Many teens dive into their cross-currents around the age of eighteen. Others do not discover their Self and never consider working with their liberation and integration processes.

What do the cross-currents look like in Jason's personality? Jason has not begun integrating his Self into his key factors, nor has he really liberated himself from unproductive factors. He is stuck in his cross-currents. The currents are pulling him in both directions without the fully engaged power of his Self. He clearly has made no significant progress with the short-term and long-term strategies I tried to teach him. Jason has cut out a lot of media and begun to read, but he still floats in cynicism. He has no direction. Most of his actions are still determined by external expectations rather than his inner disposition. Compromise after compromise is made with his parents. Emotional isolation is building up, and his anger is turned inwards. I see a lack of confidence and a lack of meaningful content in his life.

Teens like Jason may be unbeatable at the age of eighteen, but they often meet the wall when they become twenty. Why is this so? I believe the reason why teens often lose confidence and become vulnerable in a new way is because the Self takes a new step into the teen's cross-currents. The question is how much of the Self can work into the cross-currents? If the teen is able to gradually bring his Self into the cross-currents and start creating real freedom and genuine integration, he will become more and more mature as the years move on.

But kids like Jason have to start their battle with confidence all over again. His Self has emerged, but he has not connected with it. Jason is stuck in a "get off my back-don't mess with me" attitude. This attitude helps him create some freedom, but it does not give him the maturity he needs to integrate into his key factors.

As Jason's mentor at college I would look at both of his currents and assess where he stands. With Jason I would definitely appeal to his liberation current. Given his anger and pain, I think he will respond to me better if I appeal to him casting off the remains of his unhappy experience with his parents, his dullness, and the negative attitudes about people and his cultural background. The tone of his story is certainly cynical. This exposes the pain he feels due to the limited power of his Self in his daily life. His values are not clear. His multiple bad-attitudes are running away with him. I see attitudes such as: superficiality, self-criticism, introversion, and abandonment. In many ways, he has given in. Rather than developing new parts of his cognitive profile, he decides to lose himself in meaningless entertainment, alcohol, and probably drugs.

I will try to engage him in a dialogue where I put my cards on the table and confront him with the seriousness of his situation. I have to confront him but at the same time gain his trust. I ask him why he is wasting his time at college if he is so unhappy. We talk through a number of career options for him and then I challenge him to figure out where he stands.

"Just what is missing in your life?"
"If you could do five things next week, what would they be?"
"Tell me two of your most well-defined attitudes?"

The boy should be confronted with true compassion and concern. Jason has strong dimensions to access. He is a great guy with untouched passion and wisdom. But his self-destructive attitudes are too strong for his own good. By meeting him head on, something will have to give. Either he will break off contact with me, or we move into new areas of insight. If he breaks through, I will tell him about the fifteen senses and challenge him to work with his thinking and his attention every day

If he agrees to work on his thinking, I can teach him how to think with the power of his Self. I will take him through both at college.

stages of speaking for yourself as we discussed them in Chapter 10. To be honest with you, it does not look like he will ever give me that opportunity.

Should I help him create his own concept of the Self, he will reconnect with the best in himself. His positivism and love for life will come back. If I can help him look positively at the challenges he meets, he can learn overcome the coldness and randomness of his personality. It will take time for him to connect with his feelings and willpower as well!

My experience is that it is never too late for a teen. Jason has vast, untapped potential, if only he can open those doors!

Carolin is a good example of a teen approaching ideal self-development. She moves beyond the starting point her family gave her and reaches new avenues of her personality. And she does not stop there. She lives with her "edge experiences," learning from them and integrating them into her daily life. This indicates her maturity and strength. We still don't know how well she will integrate the experiences in the coming years. She will no doubt struggle, but she definitely seems like someone who will return to her core activities.

I wouldn't be surprised if Carolin headed for a crisis this fall. One difficulty now is her awareness that there is much more to life than her daily experiences. She will have to reconcile her daily reality with the vast potential she sees in herself. Luckily, she grapples with that potential to finds ways to bring meaningful content in her life. The meaningful content gives her significant opportunities beyond her daily experiences. Filling the new gap between daily experiences and the potential of her Self takes time, and it can be unsettling for many years.

Carolin searches for the truth. Childhood illusions continuously fall away as she awakens to her new potential. Her values are always in the process of being redefined. Her Self is familiar, but it is also in the process of being rediscovered. It is like meeting an old friend. What is new? The experiences of this lifetime are new, and they need to be integrated with the Self.

Carolin is strong enough to carry out her "cross-currents" honestly and consistently. Direction is very important for her. She is searching for the important people in her life. And she asks herself what she wants to do with her life in terms of work and real interests. She longs for meaningful content to her life. We see this in her willingness to work with me as her mentor.

Carolin is well on her way. She has initiated an inner dialogue between her personality in this lifetime and her true individuality. She has to continuously work hard to make this dialogue loud and clear, using her deep insight into her ideals and maturity in her social life. Her actions from the heart strengthen her moral life with each move. She will continue to struggle to make herself visible — to make a positive impact on her friends and family. Luckily, she seeks endless possibilities and shies away from confinement.

Let's talk about her cross-current processes right now. Carolin is struggling to free her Self from the shackles of her past, so I will start by appealing to her liberation current. As her mentor, I choose her relationship with her father as an example of liberating herself from the negative parts of their relationship. It is better to start somewhere and follow the progress than to fool yourself by attempting too much. She has already done some solid thinking about him and taken important steps, so it will be a good example to make the process even clearer for her. Tommy's family demons, as I explained the phenomena in Chapter 6, are still bringing her down. If she doesn't put them in the right place, they will continue to do so. She feels abandoned, and she has not yet forgiven him.

How do I work with Carolin? I start off by talking about Tommy. My goal is to help her see as many sides of her issue with him as possible: what is intentional, accidental, and habitual from his side. Then she can approach the relationship from her side: how it affects her, what she really feels in terms of anger, emptiness, etc. I always leave it up to her to make her own judgments and try to guide her into new concepts. As far as I am concerned, she doesn't need to have therapy. She is strong enough to work with this on her own, but she needs guidance.

She sets herself free if her concepts are genuine. Quite often we think we are free, but the issues are still there, and we have to work a lot more. I wouldn't place expectations on her. Progress in her liberation current depends on her genuineness.

My next step is to advise her to take a look at Gardner's framework and choose which intelligence she wants to use to unfold her senses. As you noticed in her diary, she has a strong relationship to nature and a powerful ability to experience the world through pictures. This is why she chose to go to Parsons. Visualization is a well-developed part of her cognitive profile.

Her intrapersonal intelligence is also mature, but she has a lot of work ahead if she is going to use it, to dive into her cross-currents. She should begin where she has interest and strength. Then she can branch out. For Carolin that will be her intrapersonal, visual intelligence skills. These will help her make the first steps into her cross-currents. Once she has liberated herself from some of the influences of her key factors, she can use the same intelligence skills to integrate some of her experiences in a meaningful way. Gardner's framework provides a variety of starting points. The intelligences he describes are interrelated. For example, as an artist Carolin already works daily with her spatial and musical skills. When she works on her intrapersonal skills, her logical intelligence helps her. I draw the water lily in Fig. 4 for her to enhance our conversation. Then I listen to her conclusions and judgments.

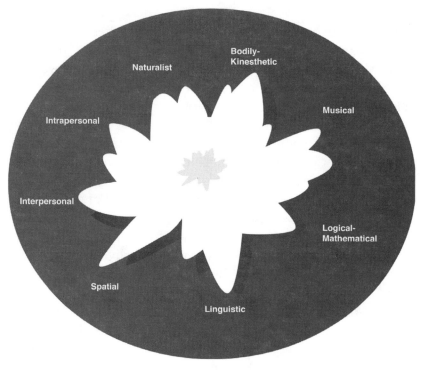

Fig. 15

Once we have spoken about the intelligences, our first conversation about cross-currents ends. Teens very quickly identify their strengths and interests in the eight intelligences.

Intrapersonal Skills

Already in my second conversation with Carolin I mention exercises that strengthen her experience of the world through pictures. They are basically concentration exercises with colors, landscapes, or with people. They help her strengthen her will by creating inner pictures of an object in nature or in the city. For Carolin they are a good introduction to her intrapersonal intelligence, and they will help her when she moves into using new senses more consciously.

We walked to a lake and agree to give each other variations on these exercises. We began with a tree. I tell her to observe it, close her eyes, and try to see it inside her mind. Then we open our eyes and correct our limited picture. She likes it. So I tell her to give me an exercise. She suggests we work on the colors in the tree. Once again we close our eyes and try to make inner pictures of the colors we had seen in the tree. The goal is to carry out the exercise as long as the Self is present. This is not easy. First, all of the daily tensions, thoughts and chaotic feelings penetrate our minds. It always takes a while before we can even start focusing on colors! We don't have to be perfect. We agreed just to start over if we fell out of the exercise.

Once we finish, we talk about our experiences. They are very different and, therefore, inspiring.

Then we work with the landscape surrounding the lake following the same simple procedure. After a couple of hours we walk back to the road and drive back to town. It will be fun to see if she continues on her own the New York City and in the country this fall. What works most powerfully — the simple exercises in creating inner pictures of nature or people with her interpersonal intelligence or the contact between us? I think it is the exercises mainly due to the fact that she creates her own exercise. This strengthens the presence of her Self. The contact between us is important but at her stage more of a secondary factor.

Once you know how to focus on the Self, it is easy to work with teenagers. And it is fun to go the depth of their cross-currents as long as you respect their inner freedom. The teacher, parent, or mentor no longer gets stuck in his or her own limited perspective but continuously get to the balcony to look with fresh vision.

The examples I have given for helping Jason and Carolin work on their cross-currents are not given as "the right way" to work with every girl or boy. They are merely examples of how I have worked with such teens. The examples are there to inspire you to find your way of working with your teens. According to your teen's interests you may work with music, sports, philosophy, hunting, computing, or whatever they are interested in! Luckily, we are all pioneers in teenage personality development. There is no universally correct approach or answer.

So far we have mostly spent time looking at the teenage years as they appear through key factors such as: the personality at this moment, cultural background and gender, parents, schooling, peer conditioning, genes, and experiences. In the following chapters I am going to share with you how I help teens use their cognitive profile to bring more of their Self into their daily lives.

PART III

The Teenage Self

Introduction

In Part III we focus on the area of teenage development that reaches far beyond their family, their nationality, their environment and the limits of their personality. We will approach the core of their personality that has become strong enough during the teenage years to create distinctiveness in their lives. There we learn to identify their new concepts, their new experiences, or their new attitudes that are formed with the power of courage, passion, and wisdom. With this power, teens not only speak for themselves, but they also tap the vast potential of their emerging Self.

No two teens are alike. Even teens within the same family end up leading unique lives. The findings of behavior genetics show that many personality traits have a genetic component. But genes cannot explain all of the varieties in people's personalities. Peer pressure, their family, and their environment also influence kids' personalities. Yet beyond their given life situation, teens show individual abilities and unique ways of thinking. They all have the power to develop their distinctiveness that lies in the power of their emerging Self. This power gives them the strength to meet the trials, the heartbreaks, and the breakthroughs that will inevitably cross their paths. It helps them navigate their own course through the chaos and the beauty of the teenage years. Just how they can use the power of the emerging Self to influence their future will be our focus in the following chapters.

Most teens are very critical of others, while being unrealistic about themselves. They know little about their own values and goals. Nor do they recognize how experiences affect them. Where they are headed in life is also largely unknown. Feelings carry them away. Teens do things they regret and have a hard time admitting failure. They breathe freedom and get out there to meet new people, to travel, to create excitement!

One of the most complicating factors in teenage development is the teen's healthy urge to slip out of the persona. If the Self participates in the actions when the teen slips out of her persona, the gap between her heart and mind does not increase. Nor will increased alienation arise. The teen reaches "edge experiences" and discovers the true core of the personality.

But if teens find ways of slipping out of their persona that prevent the Self from participating, the gap between their heart and mind widens. Such actions may be based on hate and violence, or submission to other people's will. Also, involuntary escape mechanisms in the form of stress, unreasonable competition, or cold, intellectual activity block access to the Self.

Many teens do not slip out of their persona enough. They choose to remain at the surface where everything is merely a reflection of the surrounding world, and the true content of their life often remains hidden from them. Their purpose in life remains uncertain and unattainable. If they let others tell them who they are, how they should act, and what they should be, all they will have left of personal content will be merely repetitions of what other people think. Expectations from parents and friends, as well as false mental images of themselves, will leave them helplessly swimming on the surface of their lives.

CHAPTER 12

Supporting the Emerging Self

We spend years bringing up our children with one goal—
they will be able to create the reality they want to live for. Many
teenagers do so naturally, using their inherent ability to take large
steps with simple strides. They have a mature understanding of
other people, and, most of all, they practice the art of learning
from their mistakes. Despite the odds, they use their inner
strength to create new opportunities.

Our greatest fear is that they will get stuck in their cross-
currents, not able to move beyond their starting point, and eventually drown in their key factors of personality. With this book
you are learning to focus on the emerging Self in your teens.
This source of their confidence is never easy to grasp. Due to its
very nature you are challenged to find the Self in the moment
without holding on to it. As the Self emerges, it comes and goes.
Like beauty it can not be caught beyond the moment and fixed
for the future. Nor can you find it in the past. Beauty is in the
moment, and it moves on quickly. The beautiful smile you received today from someone walking down the street towards
you no longer exists. You remember it because it warmed you
and made you feel alive, but you find it neither in the future or
the past. The glimpses you have of your teen's Self warm you
and make you feel alive; then they are gone!

When you practice focusing on the Self, you learn to understand your teen in the moment. In an instant you discover the businessman, the soldier, the merry prankster, the mystic, the artist, the rocker in your teen. It lasts for one day, and the day after you will see something new. Your teen changes before you know it.

By focusing on the emerging Self, you also learn not to be afraid of all of the hair-raising detours your teen takes, almost out of necessity. Not all of the detours affect who they are and what they really stand for. When you believe in the core of their personality, you hold the thread for them but also leave them free.

Is She Stuck in Her Personality?

One of the most common tragedies I witness occurs when teenagers and adults indulge in their personalities as a goal in itself. They reduce their personality to a tool for extreme enjoyment. In our society as a whole, the shackles of the personality are to a large degree released. Now happiness is the mainstream goal in life. Generally speaking, egotism, self-centeredness, and success remain the overriding ideals.

Many teens end up drowning in their personality — year after year. They choose to live out all of their personality traits again and again, rather than finding the next step. Life becomes a repetition, rather than a creation. This often leads to isolation and frozen thought patterns.

When you look more closely into the lives of teens that drown in their personality, one thing they have in common is that their ideals are not put into action. Without strong and independent ideals, it is very difficult to create a social life that is productive for the individual and for others.

I notice a tendency for kids to become escape artists. Their lives do not reach above the personal horizon. When they have not learned to think independently and act accordingly, it is easy to escape into a superficial role. I have seen thousands of teens waste an awful lot of time escaping down one primary cross-current stream — the liberation current. They go to extremes when using drugs, sex, money, or whatever it may be, to free themselves. Unfortunately, they totally ignore the other cross-current — the stream that integrates the Self into their personality. The result is that they liberate to the point that they lose contact with their feelings and cannot gather their thoughts. After years of self-abuse the result is often a severely weakened identity and sense of Self. Like Jason, they hide away in their egocentric behavior rather than joining the world in a healthy way. They are stuck!

In this chapter we focus first on teen identity and then move into some of the most dramatic sides of the individuation process. Then we take a big step into the core of the personality — the authentic Self that stems from the eternal being of the individual. In this book I give the eternal being of the individual, more commonly known as the "spirit" in each teen, a new name. I call it the "youthful individuality," because it brings new content and goals for this lifetime during the teenage years.

Search Uncompromisingly for their Identity

The renowned Harvard expert on youth, Erik Erikson, defines three areas of identity — *individual uniqueness, continuity of experience, and solidarity with group ideals.* I have placed them in the powerful picture shown below.

Let us look at all three circles. The first circle, the idea of *individual uniqueness,* is a key theme in this book. It appears with the emergence of the Self. The second circle, *continuity of experience*, is an area largely ignored today. Quite a few adults I meet have already given up any sense of continuity. It just doesn't work for them. When teens penetrate into the core of their personality, or the Self, as defined in this book, their experiences have a powerful continuity. This continuity is also reflected in their identity. A well-tuned late adolescent maps out her goals in life and acts on them. This continuity gives her the security to know that her life is real. It also gives her durability in her identity.

Fig. 16

The third circle, *solidarity with group ideals,* is the goal for the individual, once she has gone through her individuation process and found her ideals and her life interests. Then she unites herself in solidarity with group ideas that respect individuals. That is the basis for a powerful social life.

Many experts relate to the self on the level of identity. They assume teens have many selves and are in need of defining true selves rather then living with conflicting selves. This is true concerning their identity, their daily self. All efforts to help teens integrate true selves in their identity are extremely important. In the Teenage Edge Theory we move a step beyond the true and false selves in the teens identity to the authentic Self at the core of their personality.

Teens Have to Lose Themselves in Order to Find Themselves

When teens search for a healthy self-image, life becomes complicated. The tough thing is that teens have to lose themselves in order to find themselves. Interestingly enough, the word individuation means "indivisible." Teens lose contact with the Self — part of them that is indivisible. The process of individuation entails absolute separation from the Self in order to develop it in a new way. Something which is indivisible must leave its totality in order to develop itself.

Let us make this easier to understand. We can put individuation in the context of an entire lifetime. In this lifetime, the teen's authentic Self must be discovered anew, now based on experiences during childhood and the teenage years. To do this teens are forced to leave the indivisible authentic Self so they can find it anew. No wonder teens have to struggle to get a handle on their lives! Becoming a separate entity brings new responsibilities. Teens learn to stand alone and face the world. Either they choose to go through the process of developing themselves, or they try to avoid it by submitting to distractions, ideologies, drugs, or any of the refined forms of destructive group activity. The question inevitably arises for all teens: "Shall I submit or shall I retain myself?"

The idols of the teenage years often tell kids to squeeze the last ounce of pleasure out of life. Teens are repeatedly told to subordinate their individual values for the valueless motives of their religion, their society, their free-market economy, or other people in their life. Some easily submit their identity to cultural trends. In the end, many teens even look like each other. The global tribe cashes in! Our teens are stuck!

But those who go through the individuation process and discover part of their true Self have a strength from which they can grow throughout their entire lifetime. This part of their true Self often appears as an ideal. It is something with which they want to unite themselves during the rest of their life. In order to find it, they have to search beyond their daily self. Remember that we defined the daily self as the identity we experience on an every day basis, but not the source of change, integration, continuity, intuitions, etc. That source is the "authentic Self!"

How do teens experience the individuation process? The brilliant Swiss psychiatrist, Carl Jung, was convinced that the Self sends letters to the ego in the form of dreams. For example, an eighteen-year-old boy named Thomas received the following letter from his Self in a dream. In his dream we can see a clear picture of the individuation process:

> I saw myself together with six friends in the city jail. They had to escape. But the only way out was to trick a guard. Before I escaped, I had to leave a part of myself in jail. I tricked the guard and escaped in a boat to freedom. But a part of me was left behind. I was forced to create my own life. So I lived off the island and learned the ways of the natural world. There I made a home for myself. One day walking by the shore, I saw a speedboat washed up on the beach. I realized I had to rebuild it from nothing. There was no guarantee that it would work. I started the motor, and it worked. I drove back to the jail in the city where I freed the rest of myself.

Thomas experiences the Self in his dream and begins taking it seriously. This dream expresses a big step in the process of integration of the authentic Self his personality. When adults acknowledge his dream, he becomes more conscious of his experiences, thereby magnifying the power of it. Unfortunately, most teens do not have adults to guide them through their individuation process, let alone acknowledge their progress. They have to struggle on their own.

Carolin experienced her Self in her daily consciousness, not in her dream consciousness. This is a big difference. Carolin actually went a step further than Thomas. She experienced a moment of awakened consciousness when she experienced her Self the first time on the beach. This "edge experience" gives her an even stronger experience of integration.

Quite often teens realize they are missing something. This is a good sign. If your teen knows she is incomplete, be happy that she is strong enough to discover this and help her search! Remember that in order to search for the Self and to find it, teens have to love the part of themselves they are missing. Unselfish love drives them! When they find an ideal that belongs to their Self, they know what they want to do. They discover it again and again in their "edge experiences." Many teens discover parts of their authentic Self when they meet other people. Others do so by reading biographies or becoming inspired by someone who has reached remarkable achievements in a professional field or a social cause. I have also met teens that approach the Self through serious work with philosophy.

The following is a turning point Tim shared with me. When you read it, I suggest you try to experience the quality of Self he is discovering:

"I was never interested in books. The first book I read voluntarily was the *Autobiography of Malcolm X* at the age of sixteen. I skipped school for the whole day in order to dive into the book. It was his ability to change that most fascinated me. How could a man go through so many difficulties and still retain himself? This was a turning point for me. I started looking for such change in myself and in all of the adults I came into contact with. My father had died two years earlier, and I awoke to the fact that Dad had not been able to turn his life around. Change became an existential motive for my actions. I started looking into the depth of life. The next book I read was *Damian*, by Herman Hesse. Then it was *The Brothers Karamazov* by Dostoyevsky that set me off on my journey."

These experiences came three years before Tim had his first conscious experience of his Self. You can already identify his drive for change as a sixteen year-old. Tim told me that his search was not easy. It took him through phases of insecurity, rebelliousness, and aggression.

Living a double life is part of going through the individuation process. Weird things happen. Kids behave in ways no one can explain. They leave home. They color their hair. They change sports or drop out all together. Whatever they did last year no longer works for them. They read strange literature and dive into political debates. You name it! They get turned upside down and inside out without even knowing what is happening.

For example, I have observed many teenagers with a deeply religious inner life plunge into total doubt concerning their relationship to God and the church. Some even call themselves atheists during their search. I have seen other teenagers completely lose their faith in their country's political system. They become so disillusioned that they stop reading newspapers and involving themselves in the issues. A cynical phase may be necessary in order to come to terms with their convictions. Trust in the world and trust in the future has to be discovered anew. They are on a quest for a solid experience of their self-worth. It is the time in their lives when they search for their own sense of importance.

You can look into the drama your teenager is going through between the ages of seventeen and twenty-one and try to see what they really are struggling with. Not much of it meets the eye. But clear signs of successful steps in the individuation process appear as:

New concepts
New experiences
New attitudes
New self-confidence
The feeling of having nothing to lose
Newfound reverence

Each time you see movement in these directions, you can be confident that your teen is progressing in her individuation process. She is slowly grasping more and more of her Self but now in direct relation to her experiences in this lifetime.

The Youthful Individuality Emerges in the Self of Our Teens

In many lectures for teens I use the picture below to approach the difference between the personality and the eternal individuality. Teens listen intently when I explain that they have, in addition to their personality, a youthful-individuality. Many people call this part of our being the spirit, the soul, or the higher self. It is the eternal individuality as it appears in the teenage years.

Fig. 17

If we do not take this factor into account during the teenage years, we underestimate our teens. The individuality brings something original and unique into this lifetime. It is anchored in the past, while it also carries the future in the form of ideals, purpose in life, and the Self. Because the potential is youthful and new, it will always meet tremendous resistance in the existing institutions, attitudes, and systems that govern the social life of any country.

When I talk with teens about this part of their being, many acknowledge it immediately. The idea of an eternal, youthful individuality seems familiar to them. Yet for others it remains a foreign language. Teens know they have more going for themselves than their personality, as it is today. They sense a core to their personality. I tell them that their personality consists of their likes and dislikes, their experiences in this lifetime, their conditioning from family, friends, and education. They can easily identify with all of this. And when I tell them that much more shines through the mask of their personality, they become even more attentive. The youthful-individuality is not limited to genetic forces, heredity, and the effects of the environment in our personality development. It is an essential factor for adults to take seriously. If they do not, who will?

Where does the youthful-individuality emerge in the teenage years? Along with the personality and the Self, the youthful-individuality emerges in the heart region. We have followed Carolin's individuality emerging through the Self and slowly working into her daily activities. Although her individuality has a long past, it is experienced anew, now in relation to the teenage experiences in this lifetime.

For example, Carolin's ideals meet the daily reality of her present life. Her challenge is to bring her ideals into the reality she meets in her town, with her friends and society. One of Carolin's leading ideals is to be a strong and independent woman with a rewarding career as an artist and graphic designer. She has stopped dancing artistically and is about to enter Parsons where she will spend the next four years training her skills in design marketing. This will give her a bachelor of business administration degree. Carolin's curriculum will include art history, studio design, marketing, computer design, fashion, advertising, and consumer behavior. In addition, she can choose liberal art studies. Of course, the people she will meet and the experiences in the city will help her make her ideal a reality.

Carolin's heart region is the center of her moral activity where she strives for the integration of her thinking and acting. She identified this as her "other heart" in Chapter 8. Now her Self takes part in the creation of motives for choosing friends, or falling in love. Practical, intellectual or artistic interests are developed in relation to the realities of this present lifetime. Between eighteen and twenty-one her Self will become so strong that it changes a small part of her personality and thereby makes room for more of the strength of her "youthful-individuality" to be active.

Here is a picture of the relationship between the youthful-individuality, the Self, and the personality:

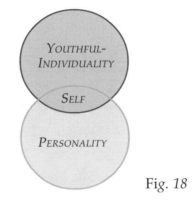

Fig. 18

This is a picture of three profound resources developing in the heart region. As adults we keep our teens covered much like wide receivers, but we cannot interfere. Our goal is not to get too close nor stay too far away. Nor can we define in precise terms what they are in the process of developing. It is new to them and new to us. Only life experience will bring it forth. That is why there is a certain form of wisdom in each individual in the teenage years. They learn from their experiences just as much or even more than adults do.

CHAPTER 13

Engaging the Sense of Self

We live with our children year after year but understand only a small part of their personality! If we engage our *Sense of Self,* we see much, much more. In this chapter I help guide your teens to engage more in their *Sense of Self.*

One Morning I Meet Jason at the Country Deli

What happens with my *Sense of Self* one Saturday morning at the Country Deli when I meet Jason and chat a bit? He is home for a long weekend from Penn State. We sit down with the other people gathered there for a good breakfast and talk about the attack on the World Trade Center on September 11. As we eat and talk, he makes an impression on me. This impression is very powerful. As a good observer, I notice that Jason dominates over me for that initial period we chat. Why? To allow him to communicate with me I naturally submit to his impression.

This is a very interesting phenomenon to step back and observe. What happens in the moment when I open myself for his impressions? Impressions release any number of feelings in the observer—for example, happiness, love, aggression, relief, etc. As I observe in the deli, my impressions of Jason release a certain feeling of sorrow. I notice that he is lost. The feeling puts me into a momentary state of sympathy. If I look closer, I notice that my sympathy for him makes me sleepy—sleepy in the sense that my Self is not fully awake as I experience Jason. The impressions he releases set me in a state of sleepy perception. I am not fully awake as I sympathize with him.

The state of sleepy perception lasts until I decide to awaken in his presence. I have submitted to his impression and thereby received a feeling. Now I protect myself from that feeling by warding it off. I decide to wake up! This demands a necessary act of antipathy in my personality. Here I use the word antipathy in the sense of taking a distance, not as a moral judgment. Antipathy is a movement in the perception that creates a distance. Sympathy is a movement closer to the impression of the other human being. I experience my *Sense of Self* when I perceive the movements of sympathy and antipathy in the moment in the deli.

When I reflect upon the experience with Jason and integrate it with other experiences, my *Sense of Self* brings these perceptions into knowledge. This is possible because my Self is not a part of my consciousness. It is a separate being that weaves in and out of my consciousness. This enables me to experience the Self of others. I do not perceive my own Self in the moment, but I experience the activity my Self carries out. I gain knowledge of Jason by cognizing the impressions I receive from him. This morning I gain knowledge of the sorrow in his life, and I naturally ask myself the question why.

The Edge Theory declares that the *Sense of Self* is both a sense and a separate intelligence that reflects upon experiences within the cognitive profile. This separate domain is a processor or reflector of all actions taken by the human being. The organ for the *Sense of Self* is the physical body — not only the brain, but also the limbs, the physical heart, and all organs. The Self becomes aware of its actions when the Sense of Self reflects upon the actions taken by the whole body. The more unconditional love the observer brings to the experience, the purer is the impression. The more unconditional love the observer brings to the experience, the richer the exchange between the Self and the *Sense of Self.*

The cycle is severely limited when driven by egotistical self-gratification.

The more egotism the person carries into the experience, the weaker the *Sense of Self* can observe the actions. Why is this so? The nature of the Self is human freedom. When inhuman attitudes and mental images filled with egotistical motives engulf the Self, the ability to use the *Sense of Self* is crippled. We see this in teens that do not learn from their mistakes. We also see it in teens that do not experience other people. They experience mere objects, not human beings.

In Figure 19 below you see how the Self and the *Sense of Self* interrelate. In this figure the Self uses the teen's cognitive profile to carry out chosen actions. With the *Sense of Self* the teen reflects upon these actions and thereby gains knowledge of how his Self acts. Why is this so significant? The healthy cycle provides self-knowledge as well as a deeper understanding of others.

Self-knowledge is much simpler than most teens realize. It comes from learning from your experiences, be they successes or failures. By using the *Sense of Self* teens develop their self-confidence. They learn from their experiences and become confident of who they are and what they do.

Subsequently, life becomes more powerful and the teens do not need to bombard themselves with drugs, media, and alcohol.

Simplified, we see that the *Sense of Self* does two things: it reflects upon our actions and thereby gives us knowledge of our Self, and with it we can experience the Self of another person.

The goal is not to remain with your own Self and feel good about it. There is much more to a healthy cycle than personal self-confidence. The social factor on a personal, national, and global level is equally important. The *Sense of Self* also allows teens to cognize the Self of other human beings as I draw in the diagram below.

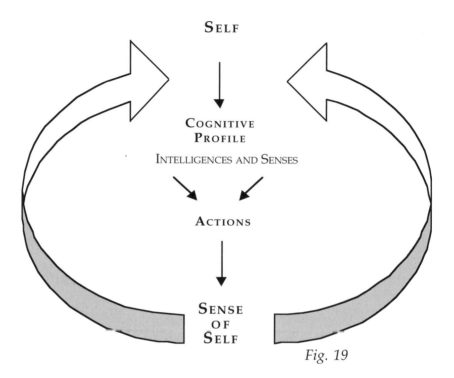

Fig. 19

By experiencing the Self of another human being, the teen extends the cycle of unconditional love to her social realities. What do our teens experience in the Self of others? Most directly they experience the other person's thoughts, deeds, and feelings. Every thought is an action. Every deed, every word spoken, is an action in the cognitive profile that is put into action and potentially reflected upon in the *Sense of Self*.

Because the Self has not fully emerged in the teenage years, the Sense of Self can be heavily influenced. Unlike the sense of sight that has the physical eye as its organ of perception, the *Sense of Self* has its emerging Self as its nonphysical organ of perception. Each time the Self receives perceptions from the *Sense of Self*, it engages more rigorously. As adults sitting on the outside, we strive to know how well the Self of our teens is engaging in his actions.

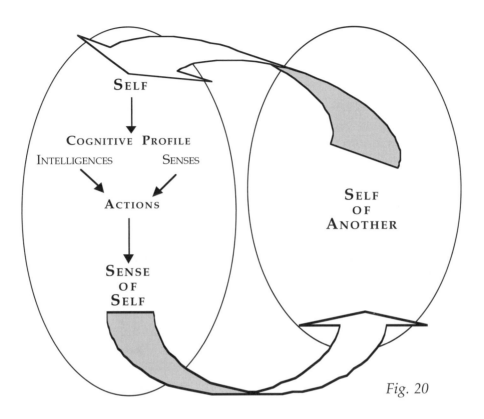

SELF

COGNITIVE PROFILE

INTELLIGENCES   SENSES

ACTIONS

SENSE
OF
SELF

SELF
OF
ANOTHER

Fig. 20

"But how can we measure the Self?" Nelson Leonard, a friend of mine from Southern California, asked as we spoke one afternoon. That is a relevant question coming from a professor of chemistry! He knows very well that the Self cannot be measured with physical instruments, but his question was sincere and open. My answer is that we measure the Self in the same way we measure intangibles such as love, laughter, and attitudes. We measure the Self according to its actions. We use our cognition and our feelings to sense the Self in ourselves and in others. We measure its presence according to the strength of the teen's ideas, ideals, and their ability to change. Where to start? I enjoy observing the presence of the Self in teens I meet daily. It is a good way to practice taking off my blinders. All I do is ask simple questions such as:

"Is she aiming for her true goals?
Are her actions one with her ideals?
Is she struggling to know who she really is?"

The Will to Act—Gaining a Healthier Sense of Self!

The clearest symptom of Jason's struggles is that he is not critical of his own thoughts. Therefore, the mental images that work in his conscious life lead a separate life of their own. This leaves him detached and easily thrown around by comments and illusions that meet him from the inside. His *Sense of Self* falls heavily under the influence of his unconscious feelings and will.

It remains passive and for long periods of time unused. If he learns how to take his *Sense of Self* seriously and share it with others, he will move forward.

I guide teens to a healthy *Sense of Self* by giving them opportunities to reflect upon their actions. This reflection is not meant to give them the introverted analysis of psychoanalytical therapy, but just the opposite. The goal is to reflect enough upon what they do with clear logical thought and thereby improve their actions. Rather than focusing on intellectual interpretations of the causes for problems, I teach teens to strengthen their will to act.

Here are three of the most direct techniques I give teens to develop their *Sense of Self* in whatever situation they are confronted with:

1. Observe the issue from as many sides as possible.
2. Discover the opposite side of the reality you face.
3. Explore the social consequences of an action.

In my opinion Jason's *Sense of Self* is temporarily disturbed, but his Self remains healthy. I want to help him engage in his *Sense of Self* so I use technique number one to help Jason work through the issues he is concerned with after the attacks on the

World Trade Center. In order to engage his Self more significantly, I want him to observe the issue from as many sides as possible. I consciously put aside my agenda in the deli and search for his points of view by asking clarifying questions. Within a couple of minutes I notice he approaches the subject from the victim's point of view, so I try to help him also consider the families of the victims and how we can help them deal with the tragedy. He becomes more and more emotional, so I listen more and then balance it with asserting new thoughts about forgiveness instead of revenge. I notice that the only way to continue the conversation before it gets out of hand is to summarize the issues we have covered and then link the perspectives to issues beyond national concern. In times of severe tragedy many people look for the positive sides to the loss they suffer, and this may be an area Jason can appreciate from different perspectives. In my last effort to keep the dialogue strong in the moment, I ask him what positive aspects can grow forth in the coming six months. Knowing a dialogue with a teen will often last no more than fifteen minutes, I drop my efforts to help him engage his *Sense of Self and* let the Saturday morning breakfast at the deli move on to other activities. These moments with teens quickly come and go, but if you have regular contact with teens, they learn from such dialogues and their *Sense of Self* unfolds.

The second technique is very powerful. The goal is to discover the opposite side of the reality he faces. For example, I can challenge Jason to figure out what he has prevented from happening by not being at Penn State this weekend? What do I expect to achieve by this? The goal is to use the power of my adult Self to help Jason engage his Self in his *Sense of Self by* digging deeper than normal into the unknown. The unknown is, of course, that which he has prevented by coming home for the weekend. Where shall he dig first? This is like losing your wallet, and you have to retrace everything you did that morning until you see the last place you placed it. In his mind Jason has to run through the opportunities he had Friday evening, Saturday, and Sunday in order to consider what he has prevented from happening. His imagination is challenged, and his feelings are initially passive, but once he touches on an opportunity he passed by, his feelings will inflame. I want to feel his feelings, for in this way I can see how they are disturbing his *Sense of Self.*

This technique is also excellent when I work with teens that complain a lot. They learn to sense some of the consequences for their actions, and it forces them to directly take responsibility for their situation rather than blaming others.

The third technique is to explore the social consequences of an action. This one will help Carolin experience the Self of others. For example, she is considering taking an internship during the summer vacation. This means she will not be able to work in Scranton. Her family will miss her, and she will not have access to the world of nature and the riding she loves in Pennsylvania. What further contrasts evolve? Just how will her family miss her? Does Erin need daily contact with her sister this summer?

By sensing Erin's Self Carolin can better understand the consequences of her action. In order to stay focused in this demanding activity, I challenge her to go through the pros and cons of her decision as thoroughly as possible. By thinking through the pros and the cons of being in NYC this summer, she can better make a decision, something teens are known to struggle with.

Good Attitudes Help Teens Engage in the Cycles!

Every day Carolin's Sense of Self easily flows into the Self of her friends. This is largely due to her good attitudes. She knows how to strengthen the flow by speaking for herself. She also thinks about her motives from time to time and, therefore, establishes more freedom in her actions. She is mature enough to learn from her previous mistakes. Her active *Sense of Self* helps her determine more and more of her personality.

As I mentioned in Chapter Three, attitudes lie deeper than habits. They determine a lot of teen behavior. And they are not easy to identify. While striving to work with the emerging Self,

I opened my eyes to the fact that attitudes are very individual no matter how much the eight key factors of personality development influence the teen. I discovered that we have great impact on teens when we help them identify their positive and negative attitudes. I always build this into my long-term strategy.

I have taught many kids from the first through the eighth grade and watched them experience tremendous changes at the age of fourteen when the emerging Self unfolds in the "other heart." Many of them struggle with serious issues that are not explainable due to parents, peer conditioning, genes, or schooling. Every day I try to understand their behavior and their needs. It is never easy. I notice some teens overcome their bad attitudes once the Self emerges, while others continue to struggle.

Jason is a good example of a boy who needs to slip out of his persona. The question is whether he slips out of his persona with the strength of the emerging Self in tact or in a destructive way that blocks out the Self. A lot depends upon his underlying attitudes and his ability to engage his Sense of Self.

To this date his parents do not see his identity crisis. Nor do they search for an understanding of his attitudes. They are irritated by the fact that he is looking for more content in his life. The only mental images Jason carries of his future are expectations coming from Alex and Sharon. Behind the scene in Jason's personality is a very destructive "Who-cares-about-poor-me–attitude!" His bad attitude surfaces as habitual self-criticism. And no one is there to help him break out of it. Does this attitude come from his relationship with his parents, or is it something he will work on his whole lifetime? I think Jason is overly self-critical not due to his parents, his peers and his schooling, but due to the fact that he has not yet grasped his Self and integrated it sufficiently. Some of the problems sit so deeply that medicine, therapy, and a positive environment provide valuable help, but the problem also has to be addressed by him.

Rely on Your Strengths

Many teens need a crisis or two before they awaken to their true strengths. When you observe a teen in a crisis, teach her to rely on her own strengths as much as possible. You have to appeal to her Self. Refuse to give in to the false self. People may say she will never make it, but she will. She can do the things they say are impossible. She can change her attitudes, take necessary risks, and strengthen her life from within. There are many hard edges to cover when the Self is awakening. It means taking control of her life existentially. Once the awakening process has begun, the need for integration of the Self becomes clear.

I worked with the parents of a girl named Vicky. They had given up on her, especially her mother. She was eighteen-years-old and caught in a cycle of self-pity and defiance. She refused to keep a deal with her parents and did her best to break down their communication. My approach to the parents was to step back from the situation and figure out which message they want to give her. They could either continue to criticize everything she does wrong, or they could show absolute confidence in her or give her every chance to prove it. The only catch was that their attitude had to be real. Their messages had to be clear, and they had to commit 100% to her. I suggested they should reserve the right to say whatever they wanted to her, and she should have the same right. The father especially understood the approach, and the mother slowly came around. Vicky started making deals with them that she respected, and the parents also proved to her that they were worth trusting. Her attitude changed, and she could use her *Sense of Self to* identify her new actions. She felt good about herself, and most importantly she could relax!

When does the Self engage in the Sense of Self?

We have all noticed that the Self does not appear on photographs. It engages in our activities. With their *Sense of Self* teens can focus on the Self weaving in and out of their social life. It appears in their work and their play. It participates in who they meet, how they interact. If we show authentic interest in their actions and try to continually observe the quality of their emerging Self, we begin to focus in the right direction.

Try to see how your teens unite themselves with things that are meaningful.

Remember that the Self engages in decision-making. It is the part of the teenage personality that creates consciousness and choice. It sets priorities, holds continuity in their actions, and displays their maturity. The Self is the teen's source of creativity — a place where they are not dependent on others. It is also the part of their personality that goes through changes.

The Self is the force with which we empathize with others — we share their suffering or their joy. With the power of their Self, they experience us, and we experience them. One of the main sources of awareness of the Self is our contact with other people. I suggest that the most powerful way we become aware of the emerging Self is by observing it in others. If teens have created a concept of the Self, as Carolin is in the process of doing, they will experience the Self more clearly working into the lives of their friends. They will see it in their parents and their teachers, as well as other adults in their life.

One of my seniors knew how to do this. She could sit in my lessons and look right through me. Whenever I noticed it, she was extremely concentrated. It startled me. Then one day we sat outside the high school building chatting, and she told me what she had seen. She had discovered some of my ideals, and she could tell me what they were! She also told me that I could focus more directly on my true strengths.

Know Their Feelings

In our buy and sell society the ability to sit by a river and feel is disappearing. Teens often go through layers of despair in order to really develop their life of feelings. They search beyond their emotions for the real experience. They want to know what is really going on! This struggle is essential to break into the feeling of Self. Only they have the key to the door. They must choose to open it up or not. Adults cannot force them. The *Sense of Self* also communicates the feeling of Self. Teens use it to reflect upon their actions and grasp the feeling in the resonance from the action. If I dance well, the feeling of the action creates a resonance and my *Sense of Self* picks it up.

Carolin is slowly becoming aware of the feeling of her Self. She knows the difference between experiences in which the Self is engaged in her actions and when it is not. If she is strong enough to stay in contact with it, she will notice how the emerging Self furthers her sense of maturity.

A Flat and Egotistical Sense of Self

What are some of the most typical symptoms of a weak relationship to the *Sense of Self*? One common symptom appears when trapped in mental images. The teen's mental images become compulsory thoughts that invade their inner freedom and cover up their power for initiative. These teens go flat and easily become egotistical.

Another symptom appears when the teen's cognitive profile is so inactive that their instincts take over. These kids are often slaves of their physical and emotional instincts. They react rather than create. Many teens that are overpowered by their instincts have a hard time experiencing other people during this phase in their lives. That is true of Jason. One side of him is predominantly superficial, and he is not comfortable with this. Another side is stiff! It is filled with egotistical attitudes with which he is protecting himself. He is trapped in his own limited, private world. Because he has such a lack of interest for others, he is becoming more and more paralyzed in his chaotic personality. This fall at Penn State we see him living out of default. He is extremely passive and cannot make decisions.

The most devastating symptom is his lack of concentration. That will take many years to overcome — if he ever wakes up at all. If his concentration problems continue for a few more years, he may even stop thinking critically and eventually lose his relationship to his Self all together.

We see a blatant polarity of symptoms in Jason. On the one hand, he can be self-destructive and remorseless. And on the other hand, he is living in illusions filled with uncontrolled feelings and a lack of judgment.

A Clear and Strong Sense of Self

One clear sign of a strong experience of the *Sense of Self* may be seen when a teen like Carolin relates to many different people honestly. She consistently speaks for herself. And she has seen herself on the edge where her Self participates in her actions. Her experience of the edge makes her search for change. Carolin is now aware of the importance of forming her thoughts with intelligent speech and writing. She finds meaningful content in her life through her experiences of nature, art, and friends.

Self-education is a free choice that she has made. She is more independent and her Self is playing a stronger role in life. With the strength of the new ideals she can slowly change certain parts of her personality. She is leaving certain attitudes and habits behind. She shows real interest in new people, the world of nature, and for the details of social life. In this way she honestly changes some of her own egotism.

In order to grasp part of the essence of the Self, teens need to overcome many of the influences of their egotistical love. The Self is, at first, a stranger to them and only their selfless love for others will give them the objective basis upon which they can recognize the emerging Self.

If the Self is not experienced by the teenager and worked with, it can become hardened and limited. The personality may become lame, because the Self is not sufficiently active in dealing with the world. Loneliness, cynicism, and retreat may become lifelong habits, when the Self does not engage with power. The personality of teenage egotists becomes drier and drier. Their inner life is impoverished.

The mentor role gains more significance as late adolescents mature, and we acknowledge their growth. No longer can we take initiatives for them. Yet we have the pleasure of supporting their self-assurance in four huge areas: unfolding their senses; integrating new experiences with courage, passion, and wisdom; and, most importantly, teenage leadership!

.

CHAPTER 14

Unfolding the Senses

Fueled by their enormous potential for sensory development, teens create new experiences every day. A number of their sensory abilities have already reached peak performance, and they have learned how to tap their individual potential. Now is the time to finely tune their sensory skills that will give them the essential competence they will need in their chosen field of work and life interests.

We see teens developing their quality of performance in all areas of life! Dancers bring their sense of *balance* and *movement* to the stage. Musicians work intensively with *touch* and *hearing*. Downhill-racers carve powerful turns at high speeds, while pushing their sense of *balance* to supreme tests. The Air Force takes five years to teach eighteen-year-old pilots how to train their senses in order to maneuver sixty million dollar F-15s, though usually nine of ten teens wash out! A teenage violinist will spend ten hours a day practicing "Tschaikowsky's Concerto for Violin and Orchestra in D major, Op. 35" in order to perform it at his debut concert. And when a class of nineteen-year-olds performs a play like *Our Town* by Thornton Wilder, a unique sensory experience streams from them to their audience. Their youthful talents can sometimes outdo even the best professional performances.

Sensory Awareness

Our teens continuously develop their sensory skills at the workplace, in cultural activities, as well as in the world of nature. The key is how much of the Self actually takes part in the activities. We can easily help teens integrate their Self into their sensory skills more consciously and regularly.

Carolin has spent the past couple of months trying to intensify this process. She wants to understand what really takes place in her senses during an afternoon walk through a Pennsylvania landscape where she meets a whole symphony of sense experiences performing for her simultaneously. On her walk, she sees the color of the sky, detects the motion of the clouds, identifies the shapes of the crowns of the trees, gauges the distance to the hills, and watches the changing speed of the swallows diving at low altitudes. The roses engage her sense of smell, as do the drying hay and the muddy lake she passes. As the sun shines through the apple trees, she feels its *warmth* on her arms, her legs, and her forehead. When she stands by a huge maple tree, her sense of *touch* is awakened by the rough bark. The crickets in the fields surround her with *sound*, and the rustling of the breeze in the trees echoes in her ears.

According to neuroscientists, all of these sense-experiences are processed separately. They are transmitted to different parts of the brain, where various senses are registered. Neuroscientists are still trying to understand how the separate sensory experiences are synthesized into the total experience of the afternoon stroll. The question is, "To what extent is she active in this process?"

Just a simple walk through a Pennsylvanian landscape brings Carolin directly into the area of science called mind-brain interaction. This area explores how our mind relates to the physical activities of our brain. If Carolin follows the "mainstream perspective," she will be convinced that her brain synthesizes all of her sensory experiences. If she follows the "edge perspective," she will realize that her Self uses her brain to synthesize her sensory experiences and that she can actively strengthen that ability.

The Self-conscious Mind Integrates and Unfolds the Senses

This poses a major question for us, "Are Carolin`s sense-experiences synthesized into a total experience by the instinctive reactions of her nervous system, or is this process of integration carried out by her Self?"

The famous neurologist, Sir John Eccles, helps us answer this question. A sudden, overwhelming experience that changed his life at the age of eighteen led him to intense studies of the mind-brain problem, and he consequently spent his life studying the neural sciences. After thirty years of brain research, Eccles became certain that we exist as self-conscious beings in a material world that includes our body and brain. The Self, as I have defined it in this book, corresponds to the self-conscious mind. Eccles states his hypothesis:

> The self-conscious mind is actively engaged in reading out from the multitude of active centers at the highest level of brain activity, namely the liaison areas of the dominant cerebral hemisphere. The self-conscious mind selects from these centers according to attention, and from moment to moment integrates its selection to give unity even to the most transient experiences. Furthermore the self-conscious mind acts upon these neural centers modifying the dynamic spatiotemporal patterns of the neural events. Thus we propose that the self-conscious mind exercises a superior interpretative and controlling role upon the neural events.[7]

The question of mind-brain interaction is a key issue for personality development in the teenage years. Just consider, for a moment, the vast areas of development that are available to a teenager who goes actively into his self-conscious being and takes part in the integration of the sensory experiences. Rather than closing the door to such creativity by assuming that the body's sets of neurons will automatically provide the integration, the teen engages her *Sense of Self to* observe the actions taken by the self-conscious mind.

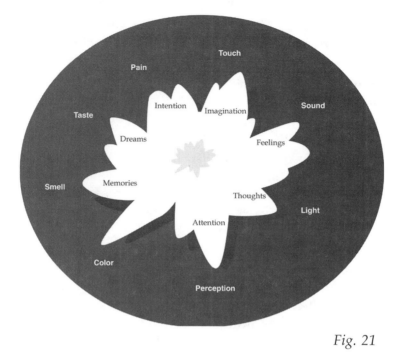

Fig. 21

The Highest Mental Experience in which a Teenager May Participate

With the self-conscious mind teens know that they know. It is the most fundamental characteristic of the teenage years. When conscious mental experiences take place over a longer period of time, they create mental unity in the teen's memory. In this way, the self-conscious mind provides continuity. "Knowing that they know" gives them confidence. The self-conscious mind further develops sensory experience and knowledge. With it teens unfold their senses.

Eccles mentions eight outer and seven inner senses that teens can work with.

I illustrate them with the image of the water lily pedals as shown in Fig. 11 in Chapter 8. When the Self emerges sufficiently by the age of eighteen, the senses become an essential part of the cognitive profile.

In this figure I have placed the eight inner senses as inside pedals and the seven outer senses as the outside pedals. They are placed randomly in relation to each other as the crown of the water lily.

Normally, we only consider five senses. Eccles names fifteen senses, but there are even more. *Movement, warmth,* and *balance* are certainly missing in this picture. The Teenage Edge Theory also includes the Sense of Self. The teenager who is conscious of her *Sense of Self* may choose to explore her inner and outer senses. With this sense she observes her actions.

Let us look into a very interesting double nature of the Self of every teenager. On the one hand, the Self is the central force in the core of the teenager's being in the "other heart" region. On the other hand, it lives, simultaneously, in the periphery. An excellent picture of this relationship may be found in the astronomical symbol for the sun.

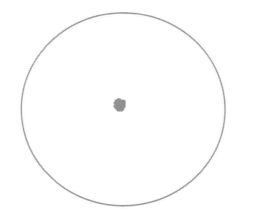

Fig. 22

The Self swings between the inner points of the "other heart" region to the bordering circle of the world. This same movement takes place when teens engage their senses of the power of the Self.

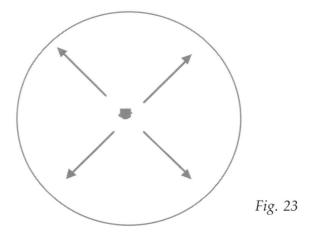

Fig. 23

The Self moves simultaneously in a centrifugal movement away from the center and in a corresponding movement from the periphery towards the center as the arrows below indicate.

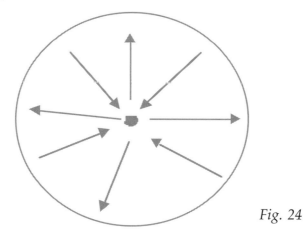

Fig. 24

Just how this movement takes place depends on the teen's activity. There can be little or no action, or there can be powerful movements. For example, master artists are able to draw in unbelievable details while including the larger picture. This reflects the power of their Self working in the focal point while also holding the periphery in their self-conscious mind. The outer and inner senses are instruments with which teens can work with the world of nature, the cities, and in their social lives. A schooling of perceptions accompanied by individual thinking with the self-conscious mind can integrate the sense-experiences and further develop their experience of the Self. This vast potential is inside all of our teens, waiting to be put into action.

New Feelings in Sound

One of the most powerful areas of productive activity for the Self in the teenage years is music. Just as the Self synthesizes sensory experiences, it also synthesizes tones into new melodies. A teenage musician uses his self-conscious mind to exercise an interpretative role. The listener and the musician use their musical intelligence to experience a melody. The cognitive profile is put into action in a process that refreshes the teen.

When teens bring their interest and enthusiasm from their Self into the sensory world, and then from the sensory experiences back to themselves, they carry out an invaluable strengthening of their personality. This process, visualized in Figure 24, helps them create inner freedom. The Self becomes clearer and clearer. It takes part in a process of sensory nourishment, which strengthens mind, soul, and spirit.

The arts become media through which they unfold their senses and develop mental hygiene. I have observed a tremendous difference between those who play an instrument or sing and those who do not work with music as children and teenagers. They often have a sense of judgment that other teens do not have. They know what it means to practice and to work hard. Musical teens learn how to judge their actions and how to live with their results. Barriers are constantly overcome due to their own initiative. Their senses are awakened and formed as skills. They develop their sense of gratitude, and I have seen how many teenagers develop their inner lives in a more distinguished way. Artistic work helps them go beyond their sympathies and antipathies. It sets them in motion. Their perception is sharpened, and, most importantly, they create new feelings.

A Walk in the Countryside

Now we observe unfolding the senses in an example from Carolin's diary.

Carolin describes her experiences in a Pennsylvania landscape. She engages her Self in multiple senses: perception, attention, light, color, feeling, thinking, and memory.

Last summer, Ted Warren challenged me to develop my cognitive profile. He helped me create my own method. In Greenwich Village I get plenty of sensory input. With my art and computer work at Parsons I work on areas such as spatial intelligence, mathematical-logical intelligence, and emotional intelligence. When I get back to Scranton, I go for walks in the woods in order to experience nature. Contemplation comes naturally for me. For most of my friends, however, it is more natural to work on their motorcycle or play basketball. In the city I watch them hit the blacktop courts and crash the boards, chase the ball and play tight defense. That is how they get the sensory input they want.

For some reason I need a regular dosage of nature. In Pennsylvania I have found some fairly untouched lakes. I like to sit on the shore of my favorite lake and focus my attention upon lily pads floating on the water. I reflect quietly and observe the flower in as much detail as possible. Then I close my eyes and try to make an inner picture of the lily. Inside my own mind, I build my inner picture of the lily. When I open my eyes again and look once more, I correct my inner picture. This is pretty simple stuff, but it works. It enables me to observe even better the next time. When I continue to observe the lily, my perception is sharpened, and I begin to concentrate even more. By looking even closer at the flower, new details arise. Then I actively engage my inner senses of *attention* and *memory* when I create a new inner picture of the flower. This is where things get more complicated — both *imagining* and *daydreaming* come into play and distract me from creating the new inner picture of the lily. I easily float off into unrelated associations.

The only way to focus again is to use my sense of *thought* to come back to the inner picture I am trying to develop. Even more senses may be drawn upon when I open my eyes again and look closer at the *colors* weaving in and around the lily on the lake. I know I am breaking through to new experiences my *perceptions* lead to new *feelings*. Subtle, but powerful new *feelings* appear.

Sometimes I wonder what the rest of the flower looks like underneath the surface. From the muddy floor of the lake the stem of the water lily grows forth in the murky waters. Down here, there are no beautiful yellow and white blossoms and petals. But life in the underworld also belongs to the radiance of the flower resting on the lily pads. Without the stem flowing from the murky underworld, the flower would never open itself to the sun. And furthermore, the single flower I am observing belongs to the whole lake, to the air, the sun, the wind, and the trees. I feel connected with the living forces at play below, upon and surrounding the lake. This reminds of the first time that I experienced my Self.

Then I try to follow the movement of my Self: from the center to the periphery of the lake-landscape and back again. In this way, I do not remain merely in a subjective experience of my senses, but the reality of the landscape gives me an objective correction. I feel refreshed!

Carolin's words speak for themselves. With that power of observation she is going places! She grasps her self-conscious mind and enters into the unfolding of her senses. This excerpt from her diary gives us a feeling for her self-reliance. I suggest you read the excerpt again and this time observe the willpower she displays in her method of experiencing nature. She engages!

Why do teens feel refreshed when they experience the wonders of nature, the joy of human contact, or the power of thought? It is because their Self has interacted with the world in a productive way. Rather than leaving the mind-brain interaction up to physical coincidences, they strengthen the flow of their Self in healthy actions.

Sensory Overexposure Makes Teens Dull

The vast majority of teenagers I meet, however, do not grasp their sense-experiences out of their self-conscious mind, but take such a distance to their natural sense-experiences that they become alienated from their senses. They spend a lot of time filling themselves up with new artificial experiences — on the screens, between the earphones, and in the urban jungle. Their artificial, sensory overload becomes a regular habit. In a bewildering variety of ways teens overdrive their nervous systems. This is one of the major reasons why teenagers lack content in their lives.

In Figure 24 we see a harmonious movement of the Self from its center to the periphery and back. When the movement of the Self from the central point to the periphery is temporarily blocked, the teenager is especially vulnerable to numerous forms of sensory overexposure. The result is a lack of integration. One example is the uncontrolled need for consumption of sensory experiences. Because their consciousness is filled with meaningless distractions, most of which are not integrated in the individual capacity for judgment, teens easy fall victim for even more stimulation. Usually they find a way to be bombarded by new mental images or sounds.

A boy in my seventh grade class started coming to school every morning more or less asleep. Michael could not wake up, let alone concentrate. His face became more and more tired. The first couple of weeks he was still friendly and cooperative. The class enjoyed their good old friend. But after three weeks Michael became irritable and aggressive. Rather than having one of the quickest minds in the math lessons, he became dull and constantly distracted. I visited him at home. His mother mentioned during our conversation that ever since the summer vacation the boy sleeps with headphones. I asked what kind of music he listened to and for how long. It turns out that Michael listened to hard rock music for an hour every night between eleven and twelve o'clock before falling asleep to the music. If the machine shut off automatically, he probably was not bombarded all night long, but one hour is enough to keep you from waking up in the morning and concentrating at school. The music was certainly not the root of his problem, but it strengthened his barrier.

If the teenage senses become ill due to overexposure, the capacity for mental awareness and feeling will be severely reduced. No healthy sense of judgment is then active, and the teen's inner life becomes weaker and weaker. The outside world no longer enriches the teen's feelings and actions. In extreme cases teens become desensitized to violence, evil, and pathological behavior due to television, films and "first-person shooter" video games.

An extreme example of sensory overexposure which devastates a teenager's energy levels may be experienced in the basement under the shiny fluorescent strobe that flashes on and off through a whirling globe during a rave party. The laser shoots light over the liquid bodies dancing in the black air. They are all looking forward to getting lost, letting go, and losing themselves in the dancing, laughter, and colored ecstasy of the party. These teenagers are out to sacrifice body and mind. When teenage hearing-receptors are under constant siege from extreme music, drugs, and modern life, many of the 32,000 hair cells in their ears stiffen because they are held too long in a rigid pose. The hair cells eventually just keel over and die. There can be no doubt that 115 decibels of heavy metal strafes the ears! After years of this and other forms of self-abuse, apparently their facial bones may become more pronounced, their teeth may rot, their brains melt, and hallucinations disorient their consciousness.

A far-reaching question any educator or parent may ask, "Is my teen receiving a healthy development of her senses?"

This question returns our attention to the exciting field of mind-brain interaction. If we take the self-conscious mind seriously, the possibility arises for schools, homes, and working places to daily promote the active participation of the self-conscious mind in all fifteen senses. In my opinion, this is necessary because so many teens need direction.

Adults can help teens break into new energy levels in two ways. One is going into the details of the actual development of all fifteen senses of the kid you are living and working with. This means asking questions like:

How is your teen unfolding her outer senses of *perception, touch, pain, taste, smell, sound, color,* and *light*?

Is she engaging in her inner senses of *attention, intention, imagining, dreams, memories, feelings,* and *thoughts*?

The picture quickly becomes very complicated, because details arise and we start looking into the reality of the teen's inner and outer sense-experiences.

The Sensory Shut Down Protects Teens

There is a very fine balance between unfolding the senses in a healthy way and falling into sensory overloads or sensory underexposure. One way of discovering how the Self relates to daily activities is to learn when your senses shut down. Teens can observe when their sensory apparatus shuts down on its own. This happens whether we like it or not. Our senses have received so many experiences that all we can do is go to sleep, feel sick, or get away for the weekend to recuperate. A shutdown is nothing new to any of us. We experience it everyday. It is a clear indicator of the fine balance between healthy and unhealthy sensory experiences.

I practice the shut down experience when I walk through a new city. As I walk down the streets, I observe how all of the impressions affect my senses. There is always a moment when an overload appears. This moment is an important experience for me on the conventional edge. It teaches me where my balance may be found. Once a teen finds the shut down moment that is peculiar for her, she has a point of reference from which to judge the abundance of energy that is always present in constructive sensory experiences and the loss of energy that is always present in constructive sensory experience. When she identifies her abundance of energy she knows more clearly her loss of energy when her Self no longer flows freely in the sensory. Teens will naturally lose their abundance when indulging in extreme activities, but if they are familiar with the lifestyle that also gives them an abundance of energy, they will find their back to it again and again.

Sensory Underexposure Limits the Personality

Are teens underexposed to certain senses? Definitely! Cecilie is a great example. I met her at a youth conference on a fjord in Norway in the village of Rosendal. There I gave a course for a week on unfolding the senses and inner picture creativity. I began the course by defining the difference between the personality and the individuality. I then gave them some simple exercises to practice while we walked that day. The goal was to observe how the senses are opened in nature and how we can create strong inner pictures of the landscape. During our first walk up the mountain, Cecile told me about the torment she had been subjected to at school for the past three years. Cecilie is an easy victim due to her inwardness. She could not find her way out of her shell, and her teachers were not protecting her. Month after month she became more and more uptight. This only gave her tormentors more pleasure from their game. Cecilie released some of the pain through dancing.

She joined our group of seven working on sensory experiences in nature for four days. We practiced engaging the Self in thinking and observation of a variety of mountain and fjord landscapes. We walked on a glacier, did concentration exercises in an English garden, and practiced placing our attention on all fifteen senses as Eccles suggested. Cecilie liked the work a lot.

After three days of working with the Self in relation to her senses and concentration, she said she had never felt so happy. She experienced that it is possible to create new feelings.

By the time a teenager has reached the age of seventeen, I believe that the individual has to unfold her senses in a process of self-education. Each teenager will have areas of her sensory life that are either underexposed or overexposed. I meet more and more teenagers who already have the maturity to discover that they can take care of themselves and further develop their sense-experiences. It is hard work. Many realize how vulnerable they are and how much of their strength has already been wasted. Many of them are interested in new experiences in nature—on the ocean, in the mountains, on the glaciers, or in the woods. Some enliven their senses through singing, dancing, or playing music. Others learn how to fly airplanes or sail boats. They know how to involve themselves.

CHAPTER 15

Courage, Passion, and Wisdom

Rushing from outer space towards the earth's atmosphere over Lake Huron to the east, it flies across the sky for a couple of seconds before suddenly exploding in mid-air. The bright object speeds gracefully towards the west in a ball of flames twice its original size! My friends and I watch the meteor shining brighter and brighter for a few more seconds before the meteor sizzles up before our eyes, about seventy-five miles high in the sky!

Like a yellow meteor racing across the summer sky, real friendships, created in the teenage years, ignite hidden sides of the individual's personality. Many teens discover that they really get in touch with their courage, passion, and wisdom when they can share it with friends. They learn to give and take in ways they never imagined. Their friends challenge them out on the edge.

Courage, passion, and wisdom stand as three pillars in the teenage years. All teens work with these awesome forces in their own way. It is a never-ending process that becomes more and more dynamic with each step forward. Integrating their courage, their passion, and their wisdom is one of the bigger tasks our teens deal with every day. In this chapter we focus on a method for seeking a balance among these pillars.

Teenage Courage Creates Opportunities

How do teens display their courage in the teenage years? They test themselves in actions on a scale anywhere between real courage and blind courage. Young, inexperienced teenagers are often hungry for adventure. They want to make their dreams come true. That may involve taking chances in nature or in the concrete jungle of the urban sprawl. They thrive on the feeling of being immortal. It is a balancing act, which they love to master. We see their displays of prowess on their snowboards, their skateboards, and in many other activities. They dance all night and play basketball all day. Some play the game of courage with total recklessness, while others develop responsibility and remain true to themselves. In border-breaking experiences they create new freedom.

Teenage Passion Engages

The yellow meteor darting across the sky at twenty-five miles per second is a very good cosmic picture of teenage passion. Like a meteor, teenage passion appears suddenly. It ignites, explodes, and then passes away. Teens engage fully in their passion with friends, on the sports field, or in the classroom. Those who are inspired spread the excitement to others. Without passion it would be very hard for a teenager to be committed to his friends, his work, or his interests. Teens base their competitiveness on passion. They create extended experiences in aesthetics, intuition, lust, or whatever it is that makes them mad, sad, or glad.

There are of course many temptations when teens have a burning desire for something. It is easy to make a mistake. But passion turns them on. It unfolds their actions. They may have an incredible passion for mischief, for heavy music, for fast driving cars, or for someone they are infatuated with. Or they may have an endless love for 26,000-ft. mountain peaks and ocean waves. In any case, they create a wide spectrum of intense feelings.

The question of control is very powerful. Teens try to stay on the edge of control while pushing that edge constantly forward. Usually they are so involved that they forget themselves and ignore the consequences. It is a game of risk. You search for real life. The new experiences may later be transformed into knowledge and good judgment from which they may encourage others. With passion they rediscover their values and intuitions.

Teenage Wisdom Gives Depth of Experience

Throughout the teenage years, our children find the friends they need to meet, the interests they need to develop, and the problems they need to work on. There comes a time in late adolescence when they need to be more conscious of their path in life. Teens strive to bring the power of their Self into their personality so they can speak for themselves. This leads to a passion for justice and respect—it is that part of them from which selfless deeds are carried out. Justice and respect are two great ideals among teens in America. Some find mentors who guide them to their ideals. Others figure it out themselves. The ideals expressed in history, literature, and religion no longer provide the engagement other generations experienced. Defining ideals is a big step for every individual—an important one to take seriously while teens have the emotional power of their teenage years!

Teens tap into their wisdom whenever they learn from their experiences and take responsibility for their job, their values. Once teens grasp some of their own ideals based on the experiences of this lifetime and forge them in a process of concept-creativity, true inner security appears. They know what they stand for. They are strong enough to grasp their courage, passion, and wisdom within their heart. Such original ideals become healthy seeds for wisdom.

What is the common starting point for all teens? Their courage, passion, and wisdom are headed in separate directions as illustrated in Figure 31 below. This challenges teens to integrate all three forces in their personality. The most direct support comes when we acknowledge our teen's progress in integrating their courage, passion, and wisdom.

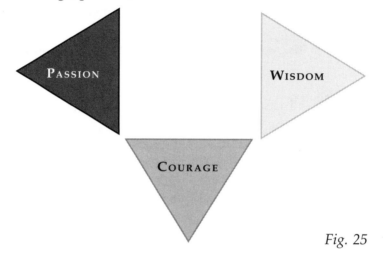

Fig. 25

All teens struggle with their courage, passion, and wisdom. Moving in their own directions, all three forces leave our teens scattered. With the power of "edge experiences" teens gradually bring their courage, passion, and wisdom into a new relationship in their personality.

Carolin and Jason

Carolin is on her way to becoming very powerful, even though her parents and friends do not see it. She is also very vulnerable. Nothing can be taken for granted. An open-hearted, open-minded teenager like Carolin enjoys life. Very often Carolin expresses herself out of insight rather than a rigid sense of duty. She does what she feels is right. In the face of pain or misfortune she has the strength to find a way to move forward. She has started to use her passion in a very constructive way. Passion for Carolin means physical and emotional fulfillment, but it also means overcoming suffering and pain. Like every other teenager she faces the naked reality of rampant destruction in the extinction of animals, the pollution of rivers, and the abuse of man. The fact that she has started to tap into her Self does not mean that she is becoming egotistical. To the contrary, she is slowly learning how to use her passion to overcome destructiveness.

True passion is much more than mischief and total engagement; it is the power with which teens overcome the separation from their Self. Their individuation process causes the separation from the Self. Their egotism is often the root of their suffering. But they do not stand still. The Self that emerges in their heart is powerful enough to turn suffering into insight. They no longer search for unlimited egotistical gratification. Instead, they search for change.

As of today Jason's courage is inactive. He has not yet identified his wisdom. And without true passion Jason will remain cynical and apathetic. He has lost direction, and he is quickly becoming the product of coincidences and commands. Because he is not learning from his lessons, he is not sufficiently tapping into his wisdom and courage. His Self comes through only in small glimpses. We can visualize his configuration of isolated passion as follows:

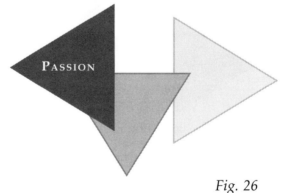

PASSION

Fig. 26

Jason's passion is clearly not engaged in the power of his courage and wisdom. He has a lot of insight and a lot of intelligence but is not bringing it into his daily life. He is not acting on his insight, nor is he brave enough to make any significant changes. His isolated passion is building up inside rather than being used creatively to meet other people, to discover his life interests, or to become an independent young man. This immaturity is common in teens that are isolated in their passion.

Just what can Jason bring into his passion in order to develop it further?

This is an important question, for either his passion will control him, or he will use it to develop his Self in a positive way. Jason needs motives for his actions that are filled with courage and individual insight. In other words, the boy's teenage passion needs to be strengthened by his courage and wisdom.

In Fig. 27 we see a picture of Jason's isolated wisdom moving in its own direction. It needs to be strengthened by his courage and passion. When he admits his mistakes and learns from his experiences new wisdom is created. When he gets rid of his putdowns, his cynicism and his censorship of others, Jason's barriers will fall and other teens will get through to him. To do so, he desperately needs to engage his courage and his passion to bring out the best of his wisdom.

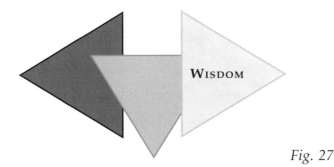

Fig. 27

Because his wisdom is isolated from the power of his courage, Jason is not brave enough to learn from his mistakes. Nor is he engaging his values in actions. He is not creating new concepts, but merely repeating what others say. The boy's intelligence leads its own isolated existence. His cognitive profile is inactive—something that is severely limiting his creativity. Thick layers of denial are building up around his heart. He lacks the passion and courage to break through his frame of reference in order to encounter new thoughts.

Isolated Courage Becomes Brutal

When courage is isolated as visualized in Figure 28 below, teens often turn cold and even brutal. There are many stages in their brutality. I meet kids who have absolutely no respect for me as a human being. They see me as another object in their way. With cold, aggressive words they manipulate the exchange to create their own advantage. In extreme cases they become the gang members, the far-rightists, and the masters of unhealthy group activities. Isolated courage is where a lot of the anger in our teens is coming from. They have "I want it now" attitudes that combine with an "I deserve it" attitude to be the motive for many violent actions. Such isolated teens live in a spiral of hate. They reinforce the self-destructive iceberg that floats below the surface of our high schools. Stupidity attracts them. Wisdom is far away, and their passion is egotistical—often hostile. Desensitized kids do not use their passion to understand and help other people. They often drown in gossip, ostracism, and plain meanness. Here is a picture of disconnected courage.

COURAGE

Fig. 28

Each "edge-experience" integrates the strength of the mature Self with the teen's courage, passion, and wisdom. In time, the ideal configuration in Figure 29 below emerges—their courage, passion, and wisdom weave coherently into their life.

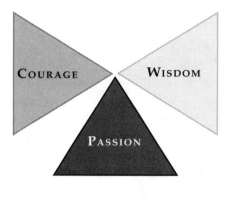

Fig. 29

It is exciting to notice when our teens bring their courage, passion, and wisdom into a meaningful relationship. With well-focused sight we can see new acts of courage, new displays of passion, and new insights filled with wisdom. These changes are present almost daily. The challenge for adults is to observe them, so the new actions may be acknowledged and thereby strengthened. Then we know our teens are stepping forward.

CHAPTER 16

Teenage Leadership

All teens want to step forward. On the outside they go off to work or college. They leave home and establish their own lives. On the inside they enter a new phase characterized by the ability of their emerging Self to create inner freedom and integration in relation to the factors of personality development. Hopefully, their work with the cross-currents will continue throughout their young adult and adult lives.

Few areas affect teens more profoundly than leadership. On one hand, teenage leadership encompasses the roles our teens play with their peers or with children. On the other hand, teenage leadership includes the way adults treat their teens. Successful teenage leadership depends on creating loyalty rather than control. It depends on honest concern for others rather than using them for one's own gain. Teens want to be recognized as individuals and treated with respect, dignity, and fairness. Young people do not want to be managed; they want to be led to think, act, and trust. They will naturally seek to eliminate hierarchy! True leadership comes from the heart, not from the boss. If our teens learn to lead genuinely from the heart, they will access vast creative resources.

It All Comes Down to Acting from the Heart

The moment of acting from the heart lasts as long as the action takes place on the "teenage edge." We can follow three clear steps in an action from the heart:

> Step 1. The teen unites herself with the idea and brings it into her personality.
> Step 2. The idea is put into action as the motive for original deeds.
> Step 3. Her actions create moral strength and give the Self more access to the personality.

We visualize three steps in actions from the heart in the following way:

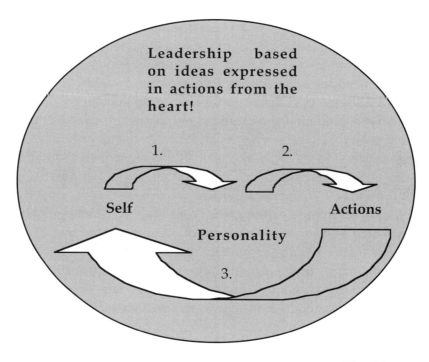

Fig. 30

Step 1. From the Self into the Personality

The teen grasps an idea and unites it with her personality. How do new ideas enter the personality? Some great scientists and thinkers work as hard as they can to free their minds of knowledge in order to find something new. Others fill their minds with as much relevant knowledge as possible. Then they evaluate the possible solutions to the problem. In this way a certain tension is built up, but we cannot force the answer. Where does the answer come from? Does it hit us when we take a walk? Or when we write down our ideas or listen to music? In any case, our ideas appear when we put ourselves in the position for a creative outburst that may become the motive for further actions. We unite ourselves with ideas and bring them into our personality.

Every day our teens grasp new ideas! One of the most exciting experiences we can have with teens is to discover when their ideas enter their personality!

Step 2. Ideas from the Personality Put into Actions

Teens engage their personality when they act on their ideas at work or in play. They take part in their actions. This is a moment in which they know where they stand. They do the work they want to do. They play the games they want to play. And they even start meeting the people they need to meet. Synchronization begins to move their life, and they now learn to trust it. The teen positions herself to be in the moment where original acts from the heart take place. Each time she acts according to her motives, she builds credibility through her actions.

Step 3. Moral Strength from Actions Streams Back to the Self

How do the actions affect the Self? Actions from the heart strengthen the teen's moral life in the core of her personality. Therefore, each action counts! With time and practice she can act consistently from the heart. The new moral strength gives the Self more access to her personality. We see this in qualities such as:

Clear judgment that sets right priorities
Consistent actions
Self-confidence and self-esteem
Continuity in conscience
Integrity and personal maturity
Productive attitudes
Values
New creative ideas

Actions from the heart are the key to sound leadership and personal growth.

Build Apprenticeships in Communities and Companies Where Hierarchy is Replaced with True Leaders

The dominating leadership programs I have noticed in business, schools, and sports are still based on Prussian or British military strategies. In my opinion they no longer support healthy leadership skills. Divide and conquer techniques, ranks, and hiding information are primitive ways of controlling people. We must take the risk of leaving these practices behind to create new leadership skills together with our teens. This means including them with more responsibility in existing schools or companies and developing modern apprenticeship programs where we learn from each other.

When I meet companies and institutions, I ask myself two questions: Does their culture foster the growth of teenage leadership and a strong sense of Self? Or does it breed the fear of failure?

In command-and-control companies we see leaders that retain a false sense of pride and security usually based on their education, their position, or their manipulation of other people. The hierarchy comfortably protects them while they spread fear to their internal competitors. They want to win at any price. Those who choose to win the battle of all against all feel justified in unlimited dominance over others.

At the other extreme I see teens that work hard to please the authoritarian who has hired them. They enjoy being repressed and do nothing about it. In these cases their obedience to authority replaces their individual liberty. All of these authoritarian activities gradually break down the individual's relationship with his Self. Without leadership showing genuine interest in others, the destruction of self-esteem spreads through the organization.

Immature Leaders Tend to Over-control and Self-destruct

Most leaders survive on their existing strengths, while ignoring the opportunities they have to liberate from and integrate with their cross-currents. When this continues into their late twenties and early thirties, only major crises will jolt them out of their patterns.

The old-fashioned leader micromanages and over-controls his people. He often hides behind his ability to speak in abstractions and his hierarchical position. By setting people up against each other and surrounding himself with "yes" men, he divides and conquers. Some even demand that teens act unethically. The narcissistic leader has made sure that he has no financial, professional, or personal accountability for his actions. Blinded by his self-importance, he avoids divergent points of view. His sense of infallibility makes it hard for him to see his own mistakes. He remains immature in his ability to work with different people.

Another technique used by old-fashioned leaders is to cultivate dependency from their teenage followers, while building abusive and manipulative relations. They place their followers in a double bind, because first the leader blames the organizational barriers, and then he blames his teenage followers for whatever does not work. Weak leaders centralize important decisions and thereby weaken the authority structure dispersed throughout the organization. They silence opposing opinions, while demanding excessive commitment. I have seen many teens that convert their best qualities to succeed in the organization.

Share the Power

When leaders use their place in the hierarchy to retain undeserved power, tremendous amounts of talent are wasted. Teens are exposed to the wrong person and will eventually lose interest in the institution. How can we share power productively in a modern apprenticeship?

In the coal mines below the hills of Pennsylvania, miners had a very strict hierarchy. If a miner started a fight down there, he would be hit on the head with a five-foot iron pipe as quickly as possible! It was too dangerous to let off steam four hundred feet under ground. On the weekends the miners in the late 19th century would gather for picnics. They wanted more human contact than sitting around their baskets could provide, so they started the game of American football. Today, when the quarterback has the ball, he is "first among equals" on a team of leaders. This is an example of leadership where the power is shared productively. On football teams leadership is shared among many leaders in the organization. They are all in it together. Otherwise they will not win.

What are New Teenage Leadership Qualities?

The Self is the power with which teens overcome the authoritarian leadership or the obedience roles they play. Teens want to understand the ways of power in their institutions, nations, and churches. They strive for knowledge of the people and the systems they deal with.

Every leader can help build self-confidence in his teens if he motivates them to feel good about themselves. New leadership initiatives are not based on force. They are created when teens act out of their love for the action! Upon such actions teens build apprenticeships with adults. The search for knowledge and the love for their actions replace the power plays of obedience and blind faith. Leadership is then based on love for the future expression of the individual.

I suggest five leadership factors to include in group activities that support high school teens creating new leadership skills:

1. Challenge them to move beyond the clique stage.
2. Value success in every field.
3. Bring out latent strengths in each person.
4. Embrace hopes and flaws.
5. Acknowledge that each teen is good at some things.

The goal is to help kids become strong enough in their personality to have solid self-esteem, which in turn allows some of them to break out of destructive group activities.

All five factors represent leadership attitudes that give teens positive support:

1. I can move beyond the clique stage.
2. My success is valued.
3. I can bring out the best in myself.
4. I embrace both hopes and flaws.
5. I know I am good at some things.

Create Security Through a Threefold Leadership Plan

In every attempt I have made to help teens connect to healthy group activities, I have worked with a three-fold leadership plan. The first aspect of belonging comes from the teen's relationship to a place, whether it is familiar hills, beaches, waters, or streets. The experience of place gives him or her a connection. In addition, kids need to connect to good people in those places!

The second factor is to help them create a realistic and strong relationship to time — past, present and future! Time gives them a good perspective on the importance of the group they are contributing to. It helps the teen see the history of the place, of the people, and of the actual group they are connected with. Good leaders consistently challenge teens to address their future possibilities. Place and time provide two essential sides of healthy group activity.

A third factor is to learn how to be strong enough to work with people who are very different from you. A healthy group welcomes individuality and dissent whether that group is composed of family, peers, neighbors, or co-workers. In order to work together and to disagree, teens have to discover the value of each other. With an active *Sense of Self* our teens will experience the Self of people who are very different from them and be strong enough to work with people who are their opposites without compromising their own unique strengths.

Learn Leadership on the Fields and in the Buildings

Our teens spend most of their teenage years in schools, on teams, or as part of companies. Leadership models greatly affect their development. The heart of leadership is mutual trust between leaders and constituents. Marvin Bower, the co-founder and former managing director of McKinsey & Company, was one of the most successful businessmen of the twentieth century. He defined four fundamental responsibilities for any leader:

1. Treat constituents with respect.
2. Develop self-confidence and self-esteem, so they feel good about themselves, get involved, take risks, and know they are worthwhile.
3. Challenge your people to take on responsibility, stretch their skills, and change their assignments.
4. Make them stakeholders of the team or institution who feel they belong, so that they learn what is going on, know the key success factors of culture, know how to deal with competition, and know how to earn profits.[8]

Bower encouraged companies and institutions to eliminate hierarchy and free up people to work more effectively and creatively. This enables them to exercise more initiative, get more ideas, and want to work together. His sixty years of consulting experience led him to believe that companies who move realistically from their hierarchical management techniques to a network of leaders would obtain higher quality decision-making, greater competitiveness and productivity, a larger share of market, and substantial improvement.

He developed methods to identify human qualities that are hard to change as well as personal attributes that are easier to change. He consulted leaders of many companies to define the areas in which they needed to change. His methods are valuable for institutions that work with teens. Learning on the job or at school is the most valuable leadership experience they have. There we can challenge our teens to take on responsibility, articulate strong opinions, and endorse divergent points of view.

Define New Attitudes Teens Want to Learn on the Job or at School

Qualities that Bower considers hard to change are inner habits such as instincts, desires, intentions, or attitudes. With teens we can work on the attitudes that drive a significant part of their interactions with the world. Attitudes color the way they think, feel, and act. Good attitudes give teens long-term strength. Poor attitudes sabotage their progress. Knowing your attitudes is the first step to leadership. Deciding which attitudes you want to develop over time is the next.

Attitudes are key leadership skills that our college and working teens are ready to develop, for example: sound judgment, honesty, thankfulness for what you receive, firmness, fearlessness, sacrifice, concern for others, the ability to bear failure with unbroken strength, and many, many more.

Challenge Teens to Know Their Personal Attributes

Our personal attributes or skills are easier to learn. We usually call them values and virtues. Marvin Bower suggested some leadership attributes that I consider valuable for teens to start developing: trustworthiness, unassuming behavior, open-mindedness, broad-mindedness, fairness, good listening abilities, sensitivity to people, sensitivity to situations, initiative, good judgment, flexibility, the ability to make sound and timely decisions, the capacity to motivate others, and sense of urgency.[9]

When I work with teens between the ages of seventeen and twenty-one, I teach them to exclude incorrect ideas from their mind. They learn to cultivate inner emotional balance, to distinguish illusion from reality, and to listen to contradictory views without agreeing or disagreeing. It is important for teens to let the realities they face speak for themselves and then penetrate those realities with their own thinking. Self-knowledge, perseverance, and common sense are extremely important.

Each company or school has the opportunity to define the leadership attitudes and attributes they are striving to develop, and in that way involve their teens in new leadership initiatives. This will encourage our teens to compete against themselves and not just against others. For competition is not only a win-lose situation, it can be the field upon which kids learn genuine commitment to others in productive communities and companies. Rather than using their intelligence to discover other people's weaknesses, teens learn to discover their colleague's ideas and then strive to help them realize their ideas. Your teens learn to engage in their actions, not only for their own sake, but for the sake of others.

As you put down this book, I hope your will to guide your teens to their unique strengths is strong and your ability to acknowledge their "edge experiences" is consistent. I hope, too, that you have come to share my conviction that the emerging Self provides our teens with essential aspects of their personality on the teenage edge!

Notes

Chapter 4 — Key Factors
1. Howard Gardner, *Frames of Mind*, (New York, NY: Basic Books, 1983); *Intelligence Reframed*, (New York, NY: Basic Books 1999).

2. Sir John Eccles, *Evolution of the Brain, Creation of the Self*, (New York, NY: Routledge, 1989), p. 232.

Chapter 6 — Breaking in the New Generations
3. Walt Whitman , essay "Democratic Vistas," in *Complete Poetry and Selected Prose and Letters*, (London: The Nonesuch Press, 1971), p. 707. Chapter 9.

Chapter 10 — Speak for Yourself
4. Martin P. Seligman, *The Optimistic Child*, (Harper Perennial, 1995), p.119.

Chapter 11 — Cross-currents
5. Ronald A. Heifetz, *Leadership Without Easy Answers*, (Cambridge, MA: The Belknap Press of Harvard, 1994), p.273.

6. Stephanie Morgan, "We Wear Sunglasses" in *Caliope*, the Abington Heights High School Literary Magazine, (Clarks Summit, Pennsylvania), p. 1.

Chapter 14 — Unfolding the Senses
7. Sir John Eccles and Karl R. Popper, *The Self and Its Brain*, (Berlin: Springer International, 1981), p. 362.

Chapter 16 — Teenage Leadership
8. Marvin Bower, *The Will to Lead, Running a Business with a Network of Leaders*, (Harvard Business School Press, 1997), pp. 48–53.

9. Ibid. pp. 23–46.

Recommended Reading

Popper, Karl R. and John C. Eccles. *The Self and Its Brain,* Berlin: Springer International, 1981.

Eccles, John C. *Evolution of the Brain, Creation of the Self,* New York: Routledge, 1989.

Erikson, Erik H. *Identity Youth and Crisis,* New York: W.W. Norton & Company, 1968.

Fischerkeller, JoEllen. "Everyday Learning about Identities among Young Adolescents in Television Culture," *Anthropology and Education Quarterly,* January, 1997.

Fromm, Erich. *Escape from Freedom,* New York: Avon Books, 1969.

Garbarino, James. *Lost Boys,* New York : The Free Press, 1999.

Gardner, Howard. *Frames of Mind,* New York: Basic Books, 1983.

_____. *Multiple Intelligences,* New York: Basic Books, 1993.

_____. *Intelligence Reframed,* New York: Basic Books, 1999.

Miller, Alice. *The Drama of the Gifted Child,* New York: Harper Perennial, 1998.

Oates, Stephen B. *Let the Trumpet Sound, The Life of Martin Luther King Jr.,* London: Search Press, 1982.

Pipher, Mary. *Reviving Ophelia, Saving the Selves of Adolescent Girls,* New York: Ballantine Books, 1994.

Seligman, Martin E. P. *The Optimistic Child,* New York: Harper Perennial, 1996.

Steiner, Rudolf. *The Human Heart,* lecture on May 26, 1922, GA212, Spring Valley, New York: Mercury Press, 1985.

The Teenage Edge Daily Workbook for Parents and Friends

This summary of the exercises in *The Teenage Edge* gives you direction in guiding your teen. They are nothing more than starting points. Most of these exercises are effective in everyday conversations, in school, or at work.

You may find it helpful to answer the following questions and then go back to the text to reread the exercise as it appears in the book.

CHAPTER 3 — THE EDGE

#1. The Edge Experience

An "edge experience" is determined by the Self fully engaging in the teen's actions.

To focus on this experience, select an action you take each day where you know your Self participates. Reflect upon that action. Was your Self engaged or not?

To discover how the Self works in your teen, notice an action your teen takes.

Ask yourself honestly whether or not you believe her Self was engaged in the action.

If so, what qualities accompany the action?

Now find a way to acknowledge the teen's "edge experiences."

#2. The Conventional Edge Experience

The conventional edge experiences differ from "edge experiences" because we are not sure whether or not the Self is engaging in the experiences.

Notice an action your teen takes.
Do you think she tested her physical or emotional borders?
Was her Self engaged or was it her instincts, feelings, or other people that determined her action on the conventional edge?
Now find a way to acknowledge her "conventional edge experience."

#3. Hate

Learn to identify three phases of hate.

The first phase starts when your teen consciously affects the will of others. Ask the following questions:

Does he have genuine interest in other people?

Is he mean and egotistical?

Does he enjoy using people?

In the second phase your teen develops more hate on a daily basis while learning how to systematically manipulate others.
Does he get other kids to work for him against their will?

In the third phase your teen has placed his intelligence in the service of pure hate and is now using that intelligence to prevent others from identifying him.
Does he want to hurt other people?
Is he planning to ruin the lives of other people?

#4. Eight Key Factors of Personality Development

Identify the differences between all eight key factors in your teen's life.

1. Self
2. Personality as of this moment
3. The Cognitive Profile
4. Cultural Background and Gender
5. Parents
6. Schooling
7. Peer Conditioning
8. Genes and Experience

Now focus on the ones that are most relevant for your teen in the moment and go into the details of those factors.

CHAPTER 5 — BEYOND THE STARTING POINT

#5. The Short-term Strategy for Carolin

First, you create a dialogue to gain confidence and trust. Then choose a theme to work on during the first week.

Share an experience of yours that she can relate to. Talk about parallels between her experiences and yours.

 The goal is to guide your teen to take new actions that will engage the Self in her cognitive profile. For example, challenge your teen to observe her Self on a regular basis by noticing when it enters her personality in the morning as she wakes up. When does she feel awake and present?

Now guide her to practice observing the moment when the Self enters her personality so fully that she feels full of energy.

A third area to observe is when she meets other people in the morning and notices that she wakes up even more! (See page 63.)

#6. The Long-term Strategy for Carolin

Chose the key personality factors you want to include in your long-term strategy. For Carolin I choose two factors that need to be integrated more fully with her Self: her cognitive profile and her experiences. The goal is to make the Self present as strongly as possible in these key factors.

To work on her cognitive profile I teach her a method to consciously deepen her experiences of nature. The first step is to develop a stronger power of attention. She does this by focusing on one object in nature for as long a time as possible while also trying to understand that object more and more.

I challenge her to start with an unusual activity — tuning into her horse's breathing when she is riding. She strengthens her attention by concentrating.

The next step is to unfold her senses by focusing on familiar landscapes.

She describes her experiences on pages 202 and 203. To help her work on her experiences I teach her to choose which sensory impressions she wants to expose herself to. She learns to differentiate between impressions that make her strong and impressions that make her weak. (See page 66.)

#7. The Short-term Strategy for Jason

In the first week it is critical that Jason receive both positive affirmation of his personality and a more direct confrontation. He needs to break away from his parents emotionally by taking his own personality development seriously and creating meaningful contents in his life. I challenge him to stop drinking and to write down his thoughts regularly. This will strengthen his dialogue with his *sense of Self*.

I ask him to recognize new thoughts and old thoughts as he writes. This helps him identify the crippling mental images that pop up automatically in his mind. When he sees new thoughts, he should act on them! This in turn strengthens his moral life and his Self's ability to access his personality. (See Fig. 30 on page 218.)

By slowly taking his ability to think seriously during the first week, I lead him to search for more meaningful content in his cultural background.

Now, decide your short-term strategy for guiding your teen.

Give him a simple but tangible exercise to work on. For example writing, helping others or working.

Guide him to develop his *Sense of Self* by reflecting upon these actions.

Search for meaningful content that interests him.

#8. The Long-term Strategy for Jason

I start with his strengths. He must continue to search for the core of his personality by working on his "who cares?" attitude. The technique I use is "playing back the message." Each time he talks about an issue with a certain attitude I answer him by saying, " So what you are saying is that. . . ."

This technique prevents him from avoiding the issue. When he identifies the attitudes, he eventually can let go of them.

Then I ask him to further develop his writing by imagining where he wants to be in five years.

Decide your long-term strategy by choosing which key factor you want to work with.

Define unproductive attitudes that are causing his behavior and play them back for him so he slowly identifies the attitudes.

Give him a simple but tangible exercise to work on. For example writing, helping others or working. Be creative here and try out a number of actions until he figures out what he is interested in. Here you will meet strong resistance in his willpower, but do not let him distract you in the long run.

Guide him to develop his *Sense of Self* by reflecting upon these actions. See page 74.

CHAPTER 6 — BREAKING IN THE NEW GENERATIONS

#9. Stress Exercise

Sit down with your teen and talk through your daily routines. This gives the teen a more realistic relationship to time and you build security.

For example, walk through the daily actions from the time she stands up until she gets to school. This reveals patterns in time, attitudes, and habits.

What needs to be changed?

If you are a teacher, make sure the parents and the teen agree to the new actions they take. See pages 80–81.

#10. Family Demons Exercise in Memory

This one is for the adults who live and work with teens. The exercise helps you work through your habits, attitudes, and emotional issues so you do not passed them down to the new generation.

The adult works backwards year by year into his memory to observe the influences he experienced as a child and a teen. The advantage now is that the adult Self is more powerful and present, enabling the adult to put the experiences in their proper place in his personality. Each time you come across an old experience in your memory, ask two questions:

Is this experience valuable?

Is this experience not valuable?

It may help to read the history of your times while you were a child and teen to see what affected you at certain ages.

You can also emphasize your search for the important people in your memory.

Look for your original ideas and ideals.

By placing some of the experiences in your memory in their proper place, you not only gain insight into the child and teen in you, but also you give the children you live or work with a true gift. The gift is the fact that you have worked through some of your experiences, thus liberating you and the teens from unwanted personality traits. (See pages 83–86.)

#11. Comparing Yourself to Others

Teach your teen to notice how he compares himself to others.

Help him identify how people put down others.

Teach him to compete with himself rather than competing with the best in the world. (See pages 91– 93.)

#12. Second-hand Violence

Challenge your teen to judge her media experiences actively.

Create a strong and supportive dialogue on the video games she plays or the movies she sees. This will help her better integrate her experiences.

By judging fairly and not moralizing over a long period of time you help her trust her judgment and determine more and more what she wants to expose herself to. (See page 94.)

#13. Three Steps to See Your Teen with New Eyes

Parents with blind spots in their attitudes and daily habits need to take three steps to meet their teens:

1. Admit you have blinders.
2. Be willing to take them off.
3. Toss out your old ways of relating to your teens.

Reread the five examples of adult blinders in this chapter and decide whether or not they have relevance for you:

1. The individual is not respected.
2. The pressure game gives rewards.
3. We adults are totally out of it.
4. The whole truth and nothing but the truth.
5. Preconceptions.

Formulate all five in questions that relate to you. Then define other blinders you have.

Now take the power of your own Self seriously and try to identify what is new in your teen's behavior. You do this by observing your initial mental images when you are with your teen.

Then ask your self what you really see now. What did you see during the past week and what you really know about her thoughts these days? (See page 106.)

CHAPTER 8—THREE BIG STEPS

#14. Identifying Changes in the Relationships between the Eight Key Factors

This exercise helps you visualize the changing relationship between your teen's factors of personality and the Self.

Step One:
We start with early adolescence at ages thirteen and fourteen, illustrated as a water lily in Fig. 7. All eight factors are pictured as roots of the lily below the surface of the water. (See page 117.)

Step Two:
Then we move to middle adolescence between the ages of fifteen and seventeen, as shown by the water lily in Fig. 8. The personality has surfaced while the Self has not yet reached the water level. This illustrates the emergence of the Self and the unfolding of the personality. (See page 118.)

Step three:
Finally, late adolescence is represented in Fig. 9 showing that the Self has surfaced and is now the crown of the flower working with the vast potential of the cognitive profile and the personality as it is at this moment. (See page 129.)

Visualize all three steps with all eight key factors.

CHAPTER 10 — SPEAK FOR YOURSELF

#15. Individual Exercise in Two Stages
Three steps of thinking determine the first stage. In the second stage the teen acts!
The first stage has three distinctive steps starting with making conclusions, then judging those conclusions from multiple points of view, and finally forming concepts. (See pages 142–149.)

CHAPTER 11 — CROSS-CURRENTS

#16. Liberation and Integration
Look for the most relevant of the eight key factors that move at this moment in your teen in two

streams within the personality.

Ask yourself from which key factor does your teen want to be liberated.

Where is she integrating more fully into key factors? On page 158 you can visualize the process before you go into details. See Fig. 14.

#17. Concept-Creativity

On page 161, I use the concept-creativity exercise to help Jason integrate more fully into key factors.

#18. Family Demons

Tommy's family demons, as I explained in Chapter 6, are still bringing Carolin down. If she doesn't put them in the right place, they will continue to do so. She feels abandoned, and she has not yet forgiven him.

On page 162, Carolin chooses to liberate herself from the negative influences coming from her father. I start off by talking about Tommy. My goal is to help her see as many sides of her issue with him as possible: what is intentional, accidental, and habitual from his side? Then she can approach the relationship from a new perspective: how it affects her, what she really feels in terms of anger, emptiness, etc. I always leave it up to her to make her own judgments and try to guide her into new concepts.

#19. Choose Your Intelligence and Senses

Advise your teen to take a look at Gardner's framework and choose which intelligence she wants to use to unfold her senses.

Guide your teen to use her intelligence skills to make her first steps into her cross-currents.

Once she has liberated herself from some of the

influences of her key factors, she can use the same intelligence skills to integrate some of her experiences in a meaningful way.

Draw the water lily in Fig. 15 for her.

Then listen to her conclusions and judgments. (See page 164 and 165.)

#20. Attention

On page 165, I present concentration exercises with colors, landscapes or with people. With them Carolin engages her Self in her cognitive profile and thereby strengthens her inner pictures of an object in nature or in the city. They are a good introduction to her intrapersonal intelligence, and they will help her when she moves into using new senses more consciously.

Walk to a place in nature or in a city.
Choose an object, a tree a statue, a painting, etc.
Observe the object, then close your eyes, and try to see it inside your mind.
Open your eyes again to look at the tree in reality and spend time correcting your limited picture.

Ask her to give you an exercise with a new object.
The goal is to carry out the exercise as long as the Self is present.
Just start over again if you notice you become distracted.
Once you finish, talk about your experiences. They are very different and therefore inspiring.

#21. Identify your Identity

On page 172 you look at Fig. 16, three circles of identity composition as expressed by Erik Eriksson. Here you identify three areas of your teen's identity. The first circle represents the idea of individual uniqueness. It appears with the emergence of the Self.

The second circle represents continuity of experience in daily life.

The third circle defines group ideals.

Use your teen as an example for Eriksson's theory and identify all three aspects of her identity.

Has your teen moved far enough through her individuation process to find her ideals and her life interests?

Is she ready to unite herself in solidarity with group ideas that respect individuals and create a powerful social life?

Now draw the circles with your teen and talk to her about her identity.

#22. Individuation

On page 176, I define clear signs of successful steps in the individuation process.

Is your teen expressing new concepts?

Is your teen creatinging new experiences?

Is your teen developing new attitudes?

Is your teen demonstrating new self-confidence?

Does your teen experience the feeling of having nothing to loose?

Is your teen expressing newfound reverence?

Each time you see movement in these directions, you can be confident that your teen is slowly grasping more and more of her Self in direct relation to the realities she faces.

#23. Identify the Self within the Other Heart
In Fig. 19 on page 184 a picture of the Self as it acts in the Other Heart is given for you to visualize and then identify in your teen.

CHAPTER 13 — ENGAGING THE SENSE OF SELF

#24. Your Sense of Self
Identify your *Sense of Self* in a simple conversation with a teen.

On pages 161 and 182 I explain how a teen makes an impression on me.

As a good observer, notice that he dominates over you for that initial period you chat.

Notice that in order to communicate with him you naturally submit to his impression.

Ask yourself what happens in the moment you open up for his impressions.

Which feelings did the impressions release in you, for example, happiness, love, aggression, relief, etc.? Define the feelings and try to explain the reason for the feelings.

Now explain how the feelings place you in a momentary state of sympathy.

Do you notice that you are not fully awake as you sympathize with him?

You submitted yourself to his impression and thereby received a feeling.

Now you protect yourself from that feeling by warding it off. Antipathy is a movement in the perception that creates a distance. Sympathy is a movement closer to the impression of the other human being.

Now use your *Sense of Self* to perceive the movements of sympathy and antipathy in the moment .

#25. Your Sense of Self Cycle
Fig. 19 on page 184 takes you through a simple exercise of identifying the *Sense of Self* Cycle:
1. Your Self engages your intelligence and senses within the cognitive profile—for example, you decide to engage your bodily, kinesthetic intelligence to shoot some baskets.
2. The Self takes actions—You shoot about twenty baskets.
3. The *Sense of Self* reflects upon the actions—You observe how well you shot and how you shot to see if you can improve your technique and concentration.
4. The knowledge from the *Sense of Self* flows back to the Self giving the Self a stronger presence in the personality—The next time you shoot, you have the knowledge and maybe better skills.
5. In this way teens learn from experiences, be they mistakes or right actions.

#26. Identify the Self of Another Person
Fig. 20 on page 185 takes you through a simple exercise of identifying the *Sense of Self* Cycle that experiences the Self of another person:

1. Your Self engages in the cognitive profile, for example, and you choose to engage your Sense of Self.
2. Your Self takes action, and you think about what the other person's ideas are at this moment.
3. With the *Sense of Self* your Self experiences the Self of another person, and you understand what he is thinking.

4. The knowledge and experience of the other person's Self flows back to your Self giving your Self a stronger presence in your personality. You know what he is thinking and you can act accordingly. Your Self is now better focused in your personality.

#27. Strengthen the Sense of Self
Three techniques to strengthen the *Sense of Self* are given on pages 186–188.

1. Observe the issue from as many sides as possible.
2. Discover the opposite side of the reality you face.
3. Explore the social consequences of an action.

I use technique number one to help Jason engage his Self more significantly. I want him to observe the issue from as many sides as possible.
Challenge your teen to approach as many points of view as possible.
Summarize the issues you cover and then link the perspectives to new issues.
Keep the dialogue strong in the moment and ask what positive aspects can grow forth in the coming six months.
Knowing a dialogue with a teen will often last no more than fifteen minutes, remember to end the exercise on time!

The second technique is very powerful. It challenges you to discover the opposite side of the reality your teen faces. The goal is to use the power of your adult Self to help him engage his Self in his *Sense of Self* by digging deeper than normal into the unknown.
For example, ask your teen what he prevented from happening by going to the movies last night.
Challenge him to run through the unknown opportunities he had last night in order to consider what he prevented from happening.

Notice how his imagination is challenged in this unorthodox way of thinking.

His feelings are initially passive, but once he touches on an opportunity he passed by, his feelings will enflame.

The third technique is to explore the social consequences of an action.

Help your teen find the major consequences of an action.

For example, she decides to take a job in another city. This creates more distance between her and her friends at home.

Explore what it means to her family members.

Explore what it means to her.

Explore what it means to her friends.

In order to stay focused in this demanding activity, I challenge her to go through the pros and cons of her decision as thoroughly as possible.

Once she takes the job and moves there ask her to evaluate how well she considered the consequences before she took the job.

#28. Criticize or Give Confidence?

The example with Vicky helps parents step back and figure out what message they are giving their daughter. The options are to:

1. Criticize everything they see or
2. Show confidence.

Step back from the situation for five minutes.

Ask yourself whether or not you are criticizing unfairly.

Would it be more productive to show confidence in your teen?

If so, work out a fair agreement for the situation.

The parents and the teen reserve the right to say whatever they want.

This opens the way for proving yourself worthy of more trust. (See page 190.)

#29. Three symptoms for Identifying a Sense of Self Clouded Over by an Egotistical Personality

Ask yourself:

1. Is your teen trapped in mental images from the past at this time?
2. Do her instincts dominate the actions she takes?
3. Does she show a lack of empathy?
   (See page 192.)

#30. Six Symptoms for Identifying a Strong Sense of Self

1. Is your teen able to speak for herself?
2. Does she have "edge experiences"?
3. Do you notice new meaningful content in her personality?
4. Are her language skills improving?
5. Is she able to move beyond some habits and attitudes?
6. Does she show genuine interest in people, society, and nature?
7. Add six more questions that may indicate that her *Sense of Self* is becoming stronger (see page 203-193).

CHAPTER 14 — UNFOLDING THE SENSES

#31. Identify Your Teen's Highest Mental Experiences

Observe moments where your teens are convinced they know what they know:

1. You start by following the flow of the Self as it weaves simultaneously to the periphery and back to the focal point in the heart region (see Fig. 22, 23 and 24 on pages 199 and 200).
   Just how this movement takes place depends on your teen's engagement.
   Is there little or no action? Are there powerful movements?
   Is the power of your teen's Self working in the focal point while also holding the periphery in her self-conscious mind?
2. Which outer and inner senses is she engaging? Are there senses you would like to challenge her to develop?
   If so, what activities will help her unfold those senses?
3. Is she creating mental unity in her memory? (See pages 202–203.)

#32. Sensory Overexposure

Do you notice that your teen is not grasping her sensory-experiences out of her self-conscious mind?

1. Is she taking such a distance to her natural sense-experiences that she is becoming alienated from her senses?
2. Is she filling herself up with new artificial experiences on the screens, in the earphones, and in the urban jungle?
3. Is her artificial, sensory-overload a regular habit that overdrives her nervous system?
4. Does she lack meaningful content in her personality?
5. Do you notice that the movement of her Self from the central point in her heart to the periphery is temporarily blocked, resulting in a lack of integration in her cross-currents?

6. Are your teen's senses becoming ill due to overexposure?
7. Is her capacity for mental awareness and feeling severely reduced?
8. Is her healthy sense of judgment momentarily shut down?
9. Is her inner life becoming weaker and weaker?
10. Does the outside world no longer enrich her feelings and actions?
11. Is she desensitized to violence, evil, and pathological behavior due to television, films, and "first-person shooter" video games?

#33. Sensory Shut Down Exercise

1. How does your teen protect herself from sensory overloads?
2. Observe when her sensory apparatus shuts down on its own.
3. Help her create new techniques by practicing a shut down experience together during a walk through the city or mall. As you walk down the streets, observe how all of the impressions affect your senses.
   Notice the moment when an overload appears for you or for her.
   Talk about it. Why did it happen? How does it feel? Notice how different your reactions are!
4. Use this shut down moment as an important point of reference. From it you judge the abundance of energy always present in constructive sensory experiences and then the loss of energy when the Self no longer moves freely.
5. Focus on the feeling you get when your energy levels are out of balance during a sensory overload (see pages 206–207).

#34. Sensory Underexposure

1. Practice unfolding your senses by engaging in inner picture creativity in nature.
2. Walk in the nature and create strong inner pictures of the landscape.
3. Now practice engaging your Self in thinking and observation of the variety of natural phenomena in the landscape.
4. Notice when you create new feelings. Stop to let the feelings sink in. This is the sign that your sensory underexposure is reduced.
5. Repeat the observation of the landscape and notice that the feelings do not necessarily return.
6. Start over repeatedly until you notice a new break-though.
7. This exercise is also possible in the cities as long as you focus on objects that are meaningful for you (see pages 207–208).

CHAPTER 15 COURAGE, PASSION, WISDOM

#35. Identify Your Configuration of Courage, Passion, and Wisdom

1. Visualize all three personality forces headed in separate directions.
2. Now identify the consequences of one-sided courage in your personality.
3. Identify the consequences of one-sided passion in your personality.
4. Identify the consequences of one-sided wisdom in your personality.
5. Now identify the consequences of one-sided courage, passion, and wisdom in your teen's personality.
6. Define where you can work to encourage your teen to bring all three together in a new way.
8. Does she need to integrate her courage, passion, or wisdom first?

9. Once she makes progress with one force notice how the other two change (see Fig. 29 on page 216).

Chapter 16 Teenage Leadership

#36. Actions from the Heart
In Fig. 30, page 218 we can follow three clear steps in an action from the heart:

Step 1. Notice how your teen unites herself with an idea and brings it into her personality.
Step 2. Discover when she puts the idea into action as the motive for her original deeds.
Step 3. Have actions created new moral strength and given the Self more access to the personality? Do you see new qualities such as:

She shows clear judgment and sets right priorities.
She has consistent actions.
Her self-confidence and self-esteem are developing.
She displays continuity in her conscience.
Her integrity and personal maturity are evident.
She enjoys productive attitudes.
Her values are changing.
New creative ideas are appearing regularly.

#37. Five Positive Leadership Attitudes
Can your teen answer these questions positively?
1. Can I move beyond the clique stage?
2. Is my success valued?
3. Can I bring out the best in myself?
4. Do I embrace both hopes and flaws?
5. Do I know I am good at some things?
(See page 223.)

#38. Prevailing Attitudes
   1. As an adult, define your prevailing attitudes.
      Share the ones you want to work on with your
      teens.
   2. Then help your teen define her attitudes and name
      the ones she wants to work on, for example:
      Sound judgment
      Honesty
      Thankfulness for what you receive
      Firmness
      Fearlessness
      Sacrifice
      Concern for others
      The ability to bear failure with unbroken strength
   3. Name many, many more that you are aware of!
      See page 225.

#39. Change Attributes
   1. Now define the attributes that are easier for you
      to change and share the ones you want to work on
      with your teens.
   2. Help your teen define her attributes that are
      important for her to work on. For example:
      Trustworthiness
      Unassuming behavior
      Open-mindedness
      Broad-mindedness
      Fairness
      Good listening abilities
      Sensitivity to people
      Sensitivity to situations
      Initiative
      Good judgment
      Flexibility
      The ability to make sound and timely decisions
      The capacity to motivate others
      Sense of urgency

Genuine concern for your people as human beings

3. For late adolescents I would add:

The ability to exclude incorrect ideas from your mind

The ability to cultivate inner balance

The ability to distinguish illusion from reality

The ability to listen to contradictory views without agreeing or disagreeing

The ability to distinguish what is meaningful from what is meaningless

Allow the realities you meet to speak for themselves

Self-knowledge

Perseverance

Common sense

Name many more that you are aware of!

4. You can build all of the most immediate attitudes and attributes into your short-term and long-term strategies for your teens (see page 226).

Bibliography

Blos, Peter. *The Adolescent Passage*, New York: International Universities Press, 1979.

Bower, Marvin. *The Will to Lead*, Cambridge, MA: Harvard Business School Press, 1997.

_____. *The Will To Manage*, New York: McGraw-Hill Book Company, 1966.

Coles, Robert. *The Moral Intelligence of Children*, New York: Penguin Books, 1990.

Eccles, John C. *Evolution of the Brain, Creation of the Self*, New York: Routledge, 1989.

Erikson, Erik H. *Identity Youth and Crisis*, New York: W.W. Norton & Company, 1968.

Freud, Sigmund. *The Complete Psychological Works of Sigmund Freud*, Volume XIX, *The Ego and the Id and Other Works*, translated by James Strachey, London: The Hogarth Press, 1961.

Freud, Anna. *The Ego and the Id at Puberty*, New York: IUP, 1936.

Garbarino, James. *Parents Under Siege*, New York: The Free Press, 2001.

_____. *Lost Boys, Why Our Sons Turn Violent and How We Can Save Them*, New York: The Free Press, 1999.

Gardner, Howard. *Frames of Mind, The Theory of Multiple Intelligences*, New York: Basic Books, 1983.

_____. *Intelligence Reframed*, New York: Basic Books, 1999.

Gatto, John Taylor. *Dumbing Us Down*, Philadelphia: New Society Publishers, 1992.

Gurian, Michael. *The Wonder of Boys*, New York: Putnam, 1997.

Harris, Judith Rich. *The Nurture Assumption*, New York: The Free Press, 1998.

Harter, Susan. *The Construction of the Self, A Developmental Perspective*, New York: The Guilford Press, 1999.

Hedges, Chris. *War Is a Force that Gives Us Meaning*, New York: Public Affairs, 2002.

Jung, C.G. *The Undiscovered Self*, translated by R.F.C.Hull, Princeton: Princeton University Press, 1957.

_____. *On the Nature of the Psyche*, translated by R.F.C. Hull, Princeton: Princeton University Press, 1954.

_____. A lecture in Zurich 1931 entitled, "Analytical Psychology and Weltanschauung," published in The Structure and *Dynamics of the Psyche in the Complete Works of C.G. Jung*, translated by R.F.C. Hull, London: Roultedge & Kegan Paul, 1972.

_____. *The Complete Works of C.G. Jung, Aion, Researches into the Phenomenology of the Self*, C.G. Jung, translated by R.F.C. Hull, London: Roultedge & Kegan Paul, 1978.

Kohut, Heinz. *The Search for the Self, Selected writings of Heinz Kohut 1950 – 1978*, Volume 2, *On the Adolescent Process as a Transformation of the Self*, Madison, Connecticut: International Universities Press.

Levy-Warren, Marsha H. *The Adolescent Journey*, New Jersey: Jason Aronson Inc., 1996.

Maslow, A.H. *The Farther Reaches of Human Nature*, New York: Penguin Books, 1971.

_____. *Toward a Psychology of Being*, Princeton: D. Van Norstrand Company, 1962.

Miller, Alice. *The Drama of the Gifted Child*, New York: Harper Perennial, 1997.

Neumann, Erich. *The Origins and History of Consciousness*, Princeton: Princeton University Press, 1954.

Parkin, Alan J. *Essential Cognitive Psychology*, Philadelphia: Psychology Press, Pennsylvania, 2000.

Pipher, Mary. *Reviving Ophelia, Saving the Selves of Adolescent Girls*, New York: Ballantine Books, 1994.

Pollack, William. *Real Boys*, New York: Henry Holt and Company, 1998.

Popper, Karl K. and Eccles, John C. *The Self and its Brain*, Berlin: Springer International, 1981.

Ricoeur, Paul. *The Terry Lectures, Freud and Philosophy*, translated by Denis Savage, New Haven: Yale University Press, 1970.

Seligman, Martin P. *The Optimistic Child*, New York: Harper Perennial, 1995.

Siever, Larry J. *The New View of Self*, New York: Macmillan, 1997.

Steiner, Rudolf. *The Philosophy of Freedom*, translated by Michael Wilson, London: Rudolf Steiner Press, 1979.

_____. *Theosophy*, London: Rudolf Steiner Press, 1975.

_____. *The Study of Man*, London: Rudolf Steiner Press, 1966.

_____. *The Course of My Life*, Anthroposophical Press, 1951.

Wexler, David B. *The Adolescent Self*, New York: W.W. Norton & Company, 1991.